# Praise for *Human behavior on the Internet*

"Excellent abstract"

–Reviewers, HCI International 2009 (On Conference paper in San Diego, California)

"Mr. Santosh Kalwar has shown extraordinary level of independence, autonomy and originality for an undergraduate student, the work related to his thesis has already provided scientific contribution as one IEEE journal and one HCI conference article has been accepted."

-Professor Jari Porras

"This is a really interesting idea: studying the anxiety levels of Internet users. The research compiled through the sources seems very complete as well."

–Reviewer, IEEE Potentials (On Journal article -Human behavior on the Internet)

"The work done for the thesis included versatile and challenging literature review due to multidisciplinary nature of the work"

-Dr. Sc (Tech) Kari Heikinen

# HUMAN BEHAVIOR ON THE INTERNET

# About the author

SANTOSH KALWAR was born in 1982 in Nepal and was accepted to the international Master's program on Information Technology at the Lappeenranta University of Technology in fall 2007. He has been very successful (finishing master program in 1 year and 4 months) in his studies and he has recently finished his M.Sc thesis on topic "Human Behavior on the Internet". The activity and innovation of the applicant was realized in this multidisciplinary work. The work related to his thesis has already provided scientific contribution as one IEEE journal and one HCI conference article has been accepted. Mr. Santosh Kalwar has shown extraordinary level of independence, autonomy and originality for an undergraduate student. He holds an M.Sc and B.E. degree in Information Technology and Computer Science and Engineering from Lappeenranta University of Technology, Lappeenranta, Finland and Visvesvaraya Technical University in Bangalore, India respectively. He is also the author of self published book "Nature God" and has written several Newspaper articles on truth, love and relationships. Visit the author online at **www.kalwar.com.np**

ALSO BY SANTOSH KALWAR

*Nature God*

# SANTOSH

# KALWAR

## HUMAN BEHAVIOR

## ON

## THE INTERNET

Lulu.com

Lulu.com *Self Publisher*

First published in Finland in 2008 as Master's Thesis by Santosh Kalwar

First EDITION 2009

Designed by Santosh Kalwar

ISBN 978-1-4092-5874-2

§

§   To my lovely family §

§

# HUMAN BEHAVIOR

# ON

# THE INTERNET

**MASTER'S THESIS**

Supervisors: Professor Jari Porras

Kari Heikkinen, Dr. Sc.(Tech)

Lappeenranta University of Technology

Department of Information Technology

Santosh Kumar Kalwar

Pekankatu 5 D 047

00700, Helsinki

Finland

GSM: +358 (0) 468872118

Email: Santoshkalwar@gmail.com

Home Page: http://www.kalwar.com.np

# ABSTRACT

**HUMAN BEHAVIOR ON THE INTERNET**


Thesis for the Degree of Master of Science in Technology


2008


77 pages, 20 figures, 06 tables and 05 appendices


Examiners: Professor Jari Porras

        Kari Heikkinen, Dr. Sc.(Tech)


Keywords: human, behavior, internet

In this thesis, "Human behavior on the Internet", the human anxiety is conceptualized. The following questions have guided the writing of the thesis: How humans behave with the Internet technology? What goes in their mind? What kinds of behaviors are shown while using the Internet? What is the role of the content on the Internet and especially what are the types of anxiety behavior on the Internet? By conceptualization this thesis aims to provide a model for studying whether humans show signs of less or exacerbated anxiety while using the Internet.

The empirical part of this thesis was built on new developed model and user study that utilizes that model. For the user study, the target users were divided into two groups based on their skill level. The user study used both qualitative and quantitative research methods. The qualitative research was conducted using interviews and observational analysis. The quantitative research was conducted in three iterations by using questionnaires and surveys.

These results suggest that the significance of human on using technology would be integral part of such a study. The study also suggests that Internet has lulled humans with the sense of dependency to greater extent. In particular, the results identified seven main areas of human anxiety. These forms of anxiety require further studies to encompass human anxiety in more detail.

# Contents

# SYMBOLS AND ABBREVIATIONS

## *Self Created in Italic*

| | |
|---|---|
| ARPANET | Advanced Research Projects Agency Network |
| BCI | Brain Computer Interface |
| BMI | Brain-Machine Interface |
| *CBOM* | *Cognitive brain OSI model* |
| CD | Compact Disk |
| CNPs | Cortical neural prostheses |
| CI | Confidence Interval |
| CL | Confidence Level |
| *CI* | *Cognitive Internet* |
| EEG | Electroencephalography |
| EcoG | Electrocorticogram |
| ERD/ERS | Event related synchronization/desynchronization |
| FMRI | Functional magnetic resonance imaging |
| GSR | Galvanic Skin Responses |
| HADS | Hospital Anxiety and Depression Scale |
| *HBI* | *Human behavior on the Internet* |
| IBM | International Business Machines |
| IP | Internet Protocol |
| IPTV | Internet Protocol Television |
| IAT | Internet addiction Test |

| | |
|---|---|
| *LTM* | *Long Term Memory* |
| MEG | Magneto encephalography |
| NSFNET | National Science Foundation Network |
| OSI | Open System Interconnection |
| PC | Personal Computer |
| PHQ-9 | Patent Health Questionnaires |
| *QS1* | *Questionnaires set 1* |
| *QS2* | *Questionnaires set 2* |
| *QS3* | *Questionnaires set 3* |
| *QS4* | *Questionnaires set 4* |
| *QS5* | *Questionnaires set 5* |
| RITE | Rapid Iterative Testing and Evaluation |
| *STM* | *Short Term Memory* |
| TCP/IP | Transmission Control Protocol/Internet Protocol |
| USENET | User Network |
| VoIP | Voice over Internet Protocol |
| WWW | World Wide Web |
| WAP | Wireless Application Protocol |

# LIST OF FIGURES AND TABLES

## List of Figures

**List of Tables**

# 1. Introduction

*"The creation of something new is not accomplished by the intellect but by the play instinct acting from inner necessity. The creative mind plays with the objects it loves."*

— Carl Jung

Twenty-seven years ago, Internet was like a small dog at the bottom of the application pile, fighting for recognition, today, vast numbers of people are using Web Services through the Internet. "Web science is about making powerful new tools for humanity, and doing it with our eyes open."[6] The Internet by definition is a "network of networks" which consists of nodes and transmits data by forming a packet using a protocol called IP (Internet Protocol) [7, 8] The Web or WWW is interlinked hypertext of documents which is accessible through the Internet. Presently, the future of the Web is assumed to be a Semantic Web." I have a dream for the Web and it has two parts. In the first part, the Web becomes a much more powerful means for collaboration between human. In the second part of the dream, collaborations extend to computers. Machines become able of analyzing all the data on the Web-the content, links and transactions between human and computers." [9] The Semantic Web as first conceptualized by Tim Berner's Lee has a vision which will make it possible for the web to understand expressive, presentation-independent, formalized language, in order to facilitate finding, sharing, and integration of information through intelligent agents and thus satisfy the needs of human to use web content.[10].

Today, the Internet has become a maturing, worldwide, universal network. The Development of Voice over Internet Protocol (VoIP), service to cell phones and mobile devices, Internet Protocol Television (IPTV) which delivers broadband video stream to home systems. With the technical and operational goals achieved on the horizon, Internet faces many challenges. As the reach of the Internet expands into more and more daily activities, the Internet has begun to mirror human society, with a great potential for both positive and negative consequences, yet design of the Internet does not follow social engineering principles. The downside of its social impact has attracted national, international, educational and political attention. When we are using Internet For example, Students, Researchers, Designers, Developers and those human who are connected in some way to the Internet use or more technically web use, we are always relating ourselves with others. A lot has been written in past about the negative use of the Internet anxiety, Internet addiction and full dependence on the internet is welling up [11] [12] [13] [14].The service disruption because of network faults, software bugs, administrator mistakes and version upgrade could seem less tolerable. Millions of human around the world use Internet to search, inform, find, communicate, work and play. Internet should not be only viewed as negative such as addiction and pathological nor should it be vilified. One must be aware of negative consequences of overuse of the Internet by understanding the behavior of themselves and from others. For example, communication, relationships, social involvement, networking, meetings, gatherings etc 70 % of Internet human build relationships with other human. Those whose everyday life involves more communication have more social resources—larger social networks, close relationships, community ties, enacted and perceived social support, and extroverted individual orientation, and they are likely to have better psychological functioning, lower levels of stress, and greater happiness[15]. By contrast, those who communicate little and have fewer social resources— social isolation, living alone, the absence of a close relationship, the breakdown or loss of a close relationship, low levels of real and perceived social support, and introversion— are more likely to have poor psychological functioning, to feel lonely, and to experience higher levels of depression.[12].

To investigate these possibilities, Screening of numerous literature showed that while there has been considerable research into the Internet, very few research projects have focused on Internet use, human behaviors and the outcome of human behaviors. This thesis is an attempt to build a new approach or find clear solution to the problems faced by human in daily activity using Internet. "It is not enough that we build products those functions, which are understandable and usable- we also need to build products that bring joy and excitement, pleasure and fun, and yes, beauty, to human's lives."[16]

## 1.1 Objectives of the Thesis

The richness of the human behavior and the growing availability of the technological opportunities mean no single right answer. The main research question is, "how can we address the challenges such as Internet addiction, psychology and human computer interaction it is currently facing now?" To understand the objectives, some of the questions were researched in details.

The thesis aims to find answers to the following hypotheses:

- *Do users shows increased or reduced anxiety level when using the Internet?*
- *What kinds of behaviors are shown when using the Internet?*
- *What is the role of the content?*
- *Finding types of the anxiety behaviors?*
- *How human process information at the internet interface?*

## 1.2 Scope of the Work

This thesis contributes to a new approach of study called Human behavior on the Internet (HBI), coined by author [17]. HBI is inherently a multidisciplinary area of research. It has to embrace theories of human behavior as well as the technological aspects of communication technology like Internet or World Wide Web (WWW). Internet and Web in Social settings is assumed to be same. The challenge is that such new approach of study has been introduced in this thesis but does not exit in real form.

The scope of the work includes design, implement and evaluate methods used in understanding the behavior of humans using the Internet technology. It has wide range of scope from the field of psychological perspective to cognitive science, behavioral science and communication technology. The scope is complex. However, To study human and their tasks and how to relate information to design style, human behavior theories, standards, procedures or guidelines in order to build an appropriate model of interaction with the help of some existing methods is investigated.

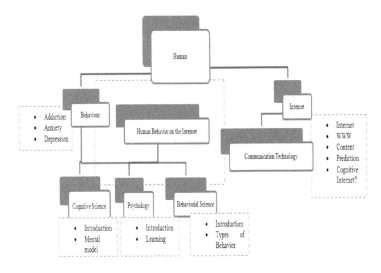

Figure 1: The figure shows a simple illustration of multidisciplinary area combined together to form a new area of research.

A small middle portion is showing HBI which demonstrates the scope of the work. Terry Winograd said, "In order to capitalize on the potential that technology has to offer, you always have to have one eye open to the question: what can the technology do?... And one eye open to the question: what are human doing and how would this fit in? What would they do with it?" The same principal is followed in defining the scope of the research.

## 1.3 Structure of the Thesis

HBI consists of five fundamental parts. Part I is the basic Introduction phase, where a concept gatherings is done. Part II is the main core part where literature collection, evaluation and filtration are done which results to Part III. In this part, comparison of various methods is carried out together with survey and design with real human in a university context. Part IV is the result phase where analysis and evaluation is carried out. Part V is the final phase to conclude the work and deserves further study.

These five fundamental parts consists of two arrows one pointing downwards and another pointing upwards. Top down and bottom up approach is followed in this thesis. The arrow on the left of the diagram is pointing down which will take us to a conclusion whereas; the arrow pointing upwards will give direction to start a research from the bottom up in near future.

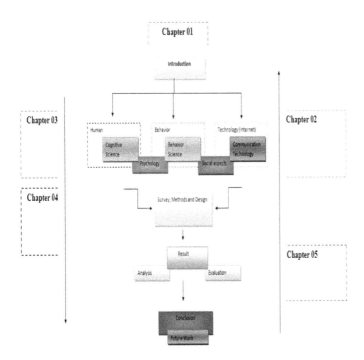

Figure 2: Structure of the Work

The Figure 2 shows predicted nature and overall structure of the work of HBI together with chapters and sub chapters that fall into its category. Right from the top of diagram through Introduction, The three single pointed arrows pointing down follows the three important keyword which are human, behavior and Internet. These three are key part of three different branch of science; cognitive, behavioral and communication respectively.

The thesis is divided into five chapters. Chapter 1 outlines the introduction, objectives, scope and structure. Chapter 2 introduces main concepts on types of behavior, human brain and Network OSI model. The purpose of this chapter is to refines the common behavior among many such behaviors used in the Internet. Chapter 3 presents design and road path for implementation of the design, based on the comparison of all the available design until date, the best suitable interaction design is proposed. Chapter 4 introduces the general implementation method based on the design. The chapter principal focus is on observation, survey, interview with focus group and questionnaires. Chapter 5 provides the analysis of the result and evaluation. Finally a brief conclusion and promising directions for the future work in new a multidisciplinary branch of science is proposed.

# 2  Cognitive Internet

*To hate is to study, to study is to understand, to understand is to appreciate, to appreciate is to love. So maybe I'll end up loving your theory.*

—John A. Wheeler

The chapter aims to answer the questions about communication technology mainly the Internet, Psychology and Social aspects of Internet Usage through the scanning of various literature reviews of research papers, journal articles and other quality literature. The chapter will briefly describe different branches of science involved in the multidisciplinary study of HBI, focusing primarily on communication technology.

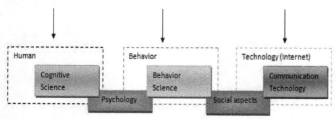

Figure 3: The purpose of chapter two: cognitive internet.

## 2.1 Communication Technology (Internet)

Communication is a process of transferring information from a sender to a receiver using a medium. Communication and information have become the basis for the world's evolving industrial society which has witnessed sweeping changes in the way we live, work and interact. On the human level, humans have to cope with more and more information and constantly changing applications of that information. Gianni Vattimo, an Italian philosopher describes the late 20th Century as the emergence of what he calls a "society of generalized communication" and has claimed that, "Everything has become an object of communication".[18]

The Internet is a medium of effective communications, flexible in cost and features, not specific to a particular piece of software or hardware and is not a single network but a group of globally collected either big or small logically connected networks. The Internet is becoming an essential environment, not only for diffusion of knowledge but also for cooperation among institutions and individuals. In developed nations the Internet has become part of everyday life. The Internet is truly an infrastructure for the information age. The Internet is not owned by any organization or any individual or any government, corporation or university. The Internet is not the same everywhere. Although the Internet has existed since the beginning of the 1960s, the most used application, the WWW is a little over a decade old. [8] One of the fascinating things about the Internet is that it comes with outstanding tools for usage in regards to recreation, education, society and much more. Current estimated statistics have shown that more than 63 million humans use the Internet in homes and the importance of the Internet in daily activities is growing. There is little which cannot be accomplished from the comfort zone of home; paying bills, research work, buying, selling, updating, uploading, downloading, shopping and, most importantly, communicating with your family and friends half way across the world. Since the establishment of the WWW, the number of Internet users has grown from an estimated 16 million in 1995 to more than 500 million in 2002 – explosive growth to say the least. [19].The rather recent but enormous and rapidly progressing emergence of the Internet has not gone unnoticed by scholars working in many different fields of research. [19] The Internet has become both an object of study and a tool of research. According to Ekhlund et al. (2003), the WWW has generated an explosion in network-mediated information exchange:

The Internet's ubiquitous nature and technical strengths, in particular, the flexible hypermedia document format and general communication protocols, have given humanity a powerful infrastructure for sharing knowledge and for interactive communication. This has created new research questions with respect to how humans conceptualize the Web, and how the use of this medium is embedded in their professional activities.[20]

A basic definition of the term host in the case of a computer network is a computer connected to the Internet. The number of hosts connected to the Internet has grown rapidly. In 1983, when the Transmission Control Protocol/Internet Protocol (TCP/IP) standard was first adopted there were only about 250 hosts connected to the Internet. By late 1993, figure had grown to two million. During 2005, the number of hosts on the Internet had increased to 317.6 million. In recent years, the number has skyrocketed to 541 million. [1] A more detailed picture is given in Figure 5 below; the picture is divided into two major columns with Millions of Hosts vs. Year. Date counting of hosts is started from 08/1981 and is shown until 01/2008. Each time the number of adjusted host count has been updated.

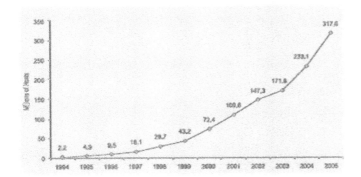

Figure 4: Millions of host on the Internet. [1]

The fact and digital data from various sources confirms that number of humans accessing the Internet is growing at a rapid pace. As the Internet evolves in terms of number of human online, it feels as if it is evolving as social community. Communities in the Internet can be compared to real life communities, according to Lazar and Preece who state; "The way humans interact in a community contributes strongly to its long-term evolution. A Human's behavior cannot be controlled but it can be influenced. The community's purpose, the human's roles in the community, and policies set-up to guide behavior, influence how humans behave. The web can support multiple forms of communication, each with its own criteria, and each with its own form of community."[21]

Worldwide, the Internet population is growing at a rapid pace. The number of people getting access to information, learning, and going online is booming like never before. It should be remembered that as late 1988, only a few countries were connected to the Internet. According to the 2004 CIA World Fact book, over 50 countries have at least one million humans using the Internet. [2]

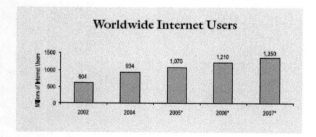

Figure 5: Worldwide Internet Users [2]

Communication has changed significantly over recent decades. Communication which once just consisted of putting pen to paper now requires just strokes of a keyboard to send mail, talk, write or even publish anything from anywhere. The concept of packet switching was developed in the Lincoln Laboratory by Larry Roberts and was used for the design of the Advanced Research Projects Agency Network

(ARPANET).[22] Just after the development of ARPANET, Intel released its first small computer. Following rapid changes in the telecoms industry, fiber optics was widely used as a communication medium. The User Network (USENET) wad used for major communications in countries like the United States, International Business Machine (IBM) and Personal Computer (PC) sales growth, the introduction of the Compact Disk (CD), and the establishment of the National Science Foundation Network (NSFNET) all started. [22] A major breakthrough came from the invention of the WWW. Gradually, larger numbers started using the WWW and Wireless Application Protocol (WAP) development took place. Increasing domain name registrations, with minor complications, were seen during the start of the 21st century. In near future, humans will have more social impact of using the Internet.

The figure below shows the history of internet communication technology, and the trend towards the predicted cognitive networking or cognitive Internet. The detailed explanation is shown in Appendix 1.

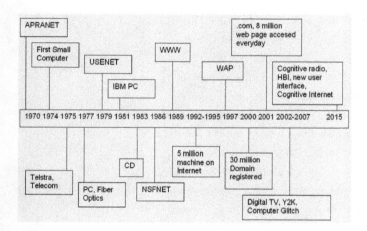

Figure 6: Time line diagram of Communication technology.

Humans once found it difficult and expensive to communicate during the times of voice telephones but with the rapid technological development communication has improved drastically. The distance has been shortened from family, friends and from seeking information which can be seen as the replacement of very important daily interactions. Boundaries of time, distance and identity are broken by the transfer of simple applications like e-mail to the complex world of virtual communities. Together with the positive growth, its negative effects are growing too. According to the U.S. Department of Justice, the Internet is an anonymous and effective way for many predators to find and groom children for illegal activities.[23] The fear of using the internet is further amplified by social disintegration, psychological and cognitive implications.

## 2.2 Social Aspect

One of the good features of the Internet applications is that they provide service by sharing information between humans with the same interests, location, or through other binding factors.

- **Community and Online Community.**

The "The Collaborative International Dictionary of English v.0.48" has about 5 different meaning of the word community, with slightly different nuances, but focusing on a common idea; a body of humans having common rights, privileges, or interests, or living in the same place under the same laws and regulations. These groups of humans share some form of social factor and these factors range from interest, experience, attitudes, race, and professions to religion, goals and locations. Wellman, Boase and Chen [24] , however, additionally described a set of essentials for a community, namely sociability, support, information, social identities, and a sense of belonging. What is an online community? Is an online community when you install community software? Is a community a group of humans? Is it when humans feel warm and fuzzy inside? It is not hard to understand what is an online community, but it is slippery to define and tricky to measure. The term "online community" is a buzz-word, especially now that e-commerce entrepreneurs are realizing that online communities can help expand their markets and bolster sales. Online social networks seem to work with the same rules as offline social networks, using community aspects and social objects in a digital environment.

- **Sociability**

In many communities either online or offline, a goal is the simple idea of being social. Sociability is necessary to the human psyche [25] ; it offers a very important basis for the other goals of the community. One good example is a bar, where humans not only come together to because of proximity, but simply to be social, enjoy themselves, have a conversation with somebody with common interests, and benefit from encounters with others.

**Support**

One feature of social networking which will be helpful in understanding HBI is support. Giving and getting support in any community, when successful, can lead to more valuable and personal relationships and through the simple need of some help to the more intrinsic value of having humans that are there for you. For e.g., the open source community like Ubuntu Operating System.

- **Information, Identity and Belonging**

Giving human technical-support includes both support and additional information on a topic. Therefore, it is necessary for many online communities to build their support around information exchange. A few communities even build their goals around the topic of information, for example, scientific communities that gather information, share, and build. One part of one's identity is the profile which is built within the community, and which can be used to extend social possibilities. One example of building such a profile is a resume that represents one's identity within the workforce community. In this case, the profile has an actual use of differentiating the identity from others, but in some cases a profile can be used for a more general goal of exploring one's identity. A sense of belonging goes hand in hand with a clear distinction of what is part and what not part of the community. Communities tend to set conditions that have to be met for members to belong. These boundaries can be setup from very physical constraint like "needs a photo camera", or more artificial ones like "needs to get invited by an existing member". Being a part of an online community is a vaguer, has looser boundaries, and consists mostly of knowing how to draw attention to yourself [26]. What makes a community successful? The question is difficult to answer because it depends on many factors and based on whose perspective success is defined. Unlike most software that serves a functional purpose, online communities are strongly social. Therefore, if we keep above ideas in mind, we can reflect the goals and effectiveness of social aspects of understanding the behavior of humans in online communities and social networks with those of general communities.

## 2.3 Social Internet Phenomenon

- **Human Web Searching behavior**

The Web searching requires a complex cognitive process model and is totally dependent on human behavior. The example studies of literature show that web search has difference in cognitive perspectives mainly in area with earlier knowledge. [27] The types of task given to a human and a cognitive style have direct influences on search behaviors. [28] Furthermore, search experience has influences on search command decisions. [29] Researchers like Holscher and Strube have explored information search behavior in different level of information searching. [30]. It has been argued that human engagement with search task is the result of personal experience in online surfing, skill level for manipulating search

- **Social Fun (Games and Porn)**

Fun is good but too much of fun has resulted in much kind of unfunny happenings. Right from addiction to various forms of Internet disorders and health hazardous issues are caused. Overuses of games have resulted in game addiction. [31] Game addiction is the result of users isolating themselves from social contact and putting all energy and efforts entirely on game achievements rather than life events.[32]. Researchers believed that players play for more number of reasons than just mere fun. Ryan, a motivational psychologist, claims that, "many video games can satisfy some basic psychological needs and often players continue to play because of rewards, freedom, and often a connection with other players".[33] Such cause can be because of the problems of antisocial disorder, depression and phobias. [33]. The overuse of game has resulted in deaths.[34] [35]. Another kind of fun could be Pornography which acts because of dependence on the Internet. Pornography is by the result of excessive reading, watching or viewing the sexual contents present in Internet.[36] Many organization and researchers have recommended content control mechanism or internet filters or censor ware, internet monitoring tool to control excessive online use of pornography [37-39, 39, 39, and 40].

- **Social behavior in the Internet (Face book, Reading news and Blogging)**

Although social networking is booming daily and human wants to form a network on the Internet. Face book addiction seems to be increasing among many humans.[41] "According to a 2006 comScore report, the average age of MySpace users is 35, with 68% of users older than age 25. Similar demographics hold true for Face book, Second Life, Friendster and Live Journal." [42] A blog is to maintain or keep the descriptions of events, happenings in an order. A political danger is always present in blogging world.[43] .An opinion posted by blogger could result in deportation from the country. One of the serious threats against blogger is possibilities of attack or threats. Although many people have mixed opinion on reading news disorder but there has been some reports on dyslexia. According to Dicman suffering from dyslexia, said." Individual who have difficulty reading and writing tend to deploy other strengths." Mr. Orfalea also pointed out that "I get bored easily and that is a great motivator, I think everybody should have dyslexia". [44] In understanding the social impact of the Internet, more study of the human brain and how the brain operates with computers are necessary. Is the Internet becoming the giant brain?

In the context of brain and behavior, is everything one does controlled by the brain? Does the human brain equal to behavior? Does the human being exist just because of the brain? Is it possible that individual brains can be connected with one another, this time via the digital language of the Internet? Is it possible to draw a practical line between the emerging Internet and any entity that we might choose to describe as living? Reverend Pierre Teilhard de Chardin, a Jesuit priest and a philosopher coined the term "no sphere", which is a "sphere of human. This sphere of human thoughts has a wide range of possibilities. Is the Internet becoming a giant brain? Ray Kurzweil and Bill Joy believe that the digital world is accelerating at such a rate that network of computers may actually become self-aware in future.

These questions have broader perspectives. Similar types of questions were once thought by nineteenth century poet, Emily Dickinson in her poem,

"With ease-and you-beside"

"

*The brain is wider than the sky, for put them side by side.*

*The one the other will contain with ease-and you-beside.*

*The brain is deeper than the sea, for hold them blue to Bue.*

*The one the other will absorb as sponges-buckets-do.*

*The brain is just the weight of God,*

*For-heft them-pound for pound-and they will differ-if they do as syllable from sound.*
" [45]


Similarly, as Douglas R. Hofstadter has so eloquently stated in the twentieth anniversary edition of his Pulitzer Prize winning book, *Gödel, Escher, Bach: An Eternal Golden Braid*, "the brain that nestles safely inside one's own cranium is purely a physical object made up of completely sterile and inanimate components, all of which obey exactly the same laws as those that govern all the rest of the Universe, such as pieces of text, or CD-ROMS or computers. Only if we keep on bashing up against this disturbing fact can we slowly begin to develop a feel for the way out of the mystery of consciousness: that the key is not the stuff out of which brains are made, but the patterns that can come to exist inside the stuff of the brain".[46]

To put social networks in perspective to off line and online communities, Together with an analysis of the techniques behind social networking, will create a better understanding of what constitutes and powers a human social network.

## 2.4 Brain Computer Interface

Brain Computer Interface (BCI) or direct neural interface or brain-machine interface is a direct communication between a human and an external device. The communication between the human brain and computer could be one way or two ways. In one way communication, the computer sends a signal to the brain or it accepts a command from the brain but not both [47]. In two way communication, the brain and computer exchange information in both directions. Neuroplasticity or brain plasticity or cortical plasticity or cortical re-mapping which are changes in brain organization as a result of experience adapts to BCI. From the area of neuroscience, the most commonly used neuroprosthetic device is cochlear implant, implanted in approximately 100,000 humans worldwide as of 2006.[48] Both neuroprosthetics and BCI are used interchangeably. BCI connects the nervous system with a computer system whereas neuroprosthetics links any part of the nervous system. Many authors have given definitions for BCI; definitions which have been tabulated below:

Table 1: Various definition of BCI

| Authors | Definition of BCI |
|---------|-------------------|
| J. J. Vidal | "The BCI system is geared to use both the spontaneous EEG and the specific evoked responses triggered by time-dependent stimulation under various conditions for the purpose of controlling such external apparatus as for example prosthetic devices"[49]. |
| J. Wolpaw et al. | "A direct brain-computer interface is a device that provides the brain with a new, non-muscular communication and control channel" [50]. |
| J.P. Donoghue | "A major goal of a BMI (brain-machine interface) is to provide a command signal from the cortex. This command serves as a new functional output to control disabled body parts or physical devices, such as computers or robotic limbs" [51]. |
| S. P. Levine et al. | "A direct brain interface accepts voluntary commands directly from the human brain without requiring physical movement and can be used to operate a computer or other technologies"[52]. |
| A.B. Schwartz | "Microelectrodes embedded chronically in the cerebral cortex hold promise for using neural activity to control devices with enough speed and agility to replace natural, animate movements in paralyzed individuals. Known as cortical neural prostheses (CNPs), devices based on this technology are a subset of neural prosthetics, a larger |

| | | |
|---|---|---|
| | | category that includes stimulating, as well as recording, electrodes."[53] |
| B. Kleber and N. Birbaumer | | "A brain-computer interface provides users with the possibility of sending messages and commands to the external world without using their muscles"[54] |

BCI is often divided into three categories: Invasive, Partially-Invasive and Non-Invasive.

1. Invasive BCI research is used to repair damaged sight and to provide new capability to paralyzed humans. Direct implantation is done into the grey matter of the brain while doing neurosurgery, which results in scar-tissue build up which in turn, causes the BCI signal to become weakened. An example would be vision BCI, in which microelectrodes is implanted into head of blind patient to allow artificial vision.

2. Partially-invasive BCI techniques are directly implanted inside the skull but outside the brain, producing lower risk of forming scar-tissue in the brain. More specifically, certain parts of the device are implanted into humans' head while other parts of the device are not. It allows better signal recognition, but is more dangerous and expensive.

3. Non-invasive BCI means that the device does not need to penetrate the skin. Electroencephalography (EEG) [49] is a

neurophysiologic measurement done through electrodes on the scalp, monitoring electrical activity of the brain. Voltages are collected by carefully putting electrodes on certain areas of the brain. These resulting voltages are used to produce an electroencephalogram which is further passed to low-pass filters and high-pass filters. Two different signals such as, electrogalvanic signals are filtered out by high-pass filter and electromyography signals are filtered out by low-pass filter. Finally, the signal is displayed on computer screen. Acquisition is done through Magneto encephalography (MEG) and functional magnetic resonance imaging (fMRI) [55] has been used as non-invasive BCI.

Figure 8 illustrates scheme of BCI, in which the brain extracts the signal for signal processing and later can be in relayed through the application interface to give feedback to the user.

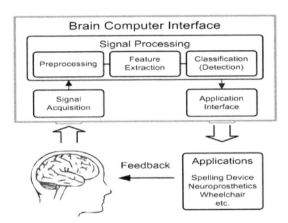

Figure 7: Scheme of BCI [3]

Most of the BCI research focuses on EEG, electrocorticogram (EcoG)[52] [56] [57] and intra cortical electrodes. [51] [53] Brain Patterns are generated by extraction of raw signals in order to produce a working BCI. Many such kinds of pattern have been employed, for example, Visually evoked potentials (VEP) [58], slow cortical potentials (SCP) [59], potentials 300 msec (P300) [60], event related synchronization/desynchronization (ERD/ERS) [61][50]and multi unit spiking patterns[51]. BCI operates in synchronous or system-driven and asynchronous or user-driven mode.[62] [63]. Experimental strategies are used such as operant conditionings [64] in which brain signals are monitored and are subject to feedback. Another strategy is called motor imagery [61] where the subject imagines the movement of muscle, for example, left and right hand movements. Feedback is used for learning where subjects adjust based on the output produced by their efforts. In BCI, skill developed by a human involves proper control of electro physiological signals which are easily adapted and modulated by the brain for better feedback.

In HBI, BCI techniques could be used for testing and analyzing different activities on the Internet.

## 2.5 Psychology and Cognitive Science

Psychology started as an independent study during 1879 by founder Wilhelm Wundt who is known as the "father of psychology". [65] Since the beginning of the 1980s, psychology has begun to examine the relationship between consciousness and the brain. Psychology is an attempt to explain consciousness, behavior, social interaction, personality, emotions, cognition and perception. Psychology refers to knowledge of daily activity. [66] One type of psychological study is neuropsychology, which is the study of the brain in relation to specific psychological processes and open behaviors. Minsky, who first developed the Society of Mind theory, has demonstrated that "mind is what brains do". His theory views mind as the evolution of cognitive systems which are a society of individual simple processes called agents. The idea is best illustrated by the following quote. "What magical trick makes us intelligent? The trick is that there is no trick. The power of intelligence stems from our vast diversity, not from any single, perfect principle."[67] Cognitive Science is an interdisciplinary branch of science coined by Christopher Longuet-Higgins in 1973 and is the study of mind or intelligence. [88] Cognition is the process of gaining knowledge by understanding, remembering, reasoning, attending, being aware and creating new ideas. "One major contribution of both Artificial Intelligence and Cognitive Science to Psychology has been the information processing model of human thinking in which the metaphor of "brain-as-computer" is taken quite literally."[68]. Attention, language processing, learning and development, and memory are key terms used in Cognitive Science.. Cognitive psychology, social knowledge and organizational knowledge could help to improve the technology, systems and applications in the Internet together with the understanding of human behavior with respect to action and reaction to the environment. Research has shown certain social groups to be under-represented on the Internet [69] [70] [71] [72] not simply because of a lack of access, but more because of cognitive, motivational and affective factors [73]. Psychology therefore has an important role in advancing the understanding of why humans choose to use or not to choose the usage of the Internet [74]. There will always be an argument to model psychology with technology or technology with psychology however; combining psychology with technology will give rise to new technology called psycho technology.

## 2.6 Human Computer Interaction

Humans are subject to lapses in concentration, motivation factors, emotions, fear, errors, change in mood and misjudgments, but at the same time they are also capable of remarkable feats, co-perceiving and responding quickly to external stimuli, coordinating various actions, creating masterpieces and solving complex problems. The ethnographic study of the Internet can be divided into two categories. First, user-based and second, content based. User-based analysis is about the investigation, examination and the study of humans using the Internet. Whereas, content based analysis is mainly focused on text. Humans are capable of providing reasons to support their points of view if asked a question such as "What color is my shirt?" and are capable of knowing without explicit Deduction or reasoning answers to questions like, "If I were you, I would hate myself", whereas computers cannot function without specific programming instructions. Human brain is highly capable of processing information not just binary number processing as of today's computers. Everything that a human senses through sight, hearing, touch, smell and taste is processed as information in the mind. The basic idea is that information enters and exits the mind through a series of ordered processing stages.[75]

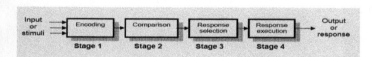

Figure 8: Human information processing stages. [30]

However, there is growing concern to understand human's need in which they are operated. As said by Winograd and Flores in 1986, "It is clear that (and has been widely recognized) that one cannot understand a technology without having a functional understanding of how it is used. Furthermore, that understanding must incorporate a holistic view of the network of technologies and activities into which it fits, rather than treating the technological devices in isolation." Human interaction could be recognized in a cognitive perspective by conceptualizing physically, the human brain and behavior in more detail to nderstand HBI..

## 2.7 Discussion

In the networking OSI model, the top layer is the application layer. The major Internet protocols are used at the top of the Application layer, for example, http, https, ftps etc. When using the Internet, any patterns of behavior generated by humans are on top of this layer. Even though, brain is much more complex in working than the network Open System Interconnection (OSI) model there could be some similarities in them. The human brain's Central nervous system which could be divided into seven main parts:

1. The first part is *spinal cord* which receives and processes sensory information from skin, joints and muscles of the limbs.
2. Second part is *medulla oblongata* which lies directly above spinal cord which is responsible for digestion, breathing and control of heart rate.
3. Third part which lies above medulla is *Pons* which is responsible for conveying information from cerebral hemisphere to cerebellum.
4. Fourth part lies behind Pons called *cerebellum* which is connected to brain stem by several major fiber tracts called peduncles. It ranges movement and is involved in the learning of motor skills.
5. Fifth part which lies rostral to the Pons is *midbrain* which coordinates much sensory and motor function, including eye movement and coordination of visual and auditory reflexes.

6. Sixth part *diencephalons* lies rostral to midbrain which has two structure first thalamus, processes information reaching to cerebral cortex from the rest of central nervous system and hypothalamus, regulates autonomic, endocrine and visceral functions.

7. Seventh part *cerebral hemisphere* which is wrinkled outer layer consists of three deep structure, basal ganglia, hippo campus and amygdaloidal nuclei.

The cerebral cortex could be divided into four lobes: frontal, parietal, temporal and occipital.

- The *frontal lobe* is responsible with planning future action and with control of movement;
- The *parietal lobe* with somatic sensation, with forming body image, and with relating one's body image with extra personal space;
- *occipital lobe* with vision;
- *Temporal lobe* with hearing.

In a network, the OSI model consists of seven layers.

1. The physical layer transmits only raw bits where electrical signals are being transmitted similar to brain processing signals after the observation of the environment. In the brain, this could be analogous to the *spinal cord*, which receives and processes sensory information from skin, joints and muscles of the limbs.

2. The data link layer transmits packets from node to node based on station addresses similar to observations of physical body parts such as eyes or hands or ears. In the brain, this could be similar to the *medulla oblongata*.

3. In the case of the network layer, the data are routed in the network based on the address. In the brain, this could be seen as the cerebellum, which is connected to the brain stem by several major fiber tracts called *peduncles*.

4. The transport layer ensures the delivery of the file or message where the organs involved after observation of an object transmit the signal or message to the appropriate region. In the brain, this could be the *Pons* which is responsible for conveying information from the cerebral hemisphere to the cerebellum.

5. The session layer starts, stops, and maintains the order of the session. In the brain, storing information, retrieving information and ignoring it if it is not needed is part of the work of the *cerebellum*, which is connected to brain stem by several major fiber tracts called *peduncles*.

6. The presentation layer does encryption and data conversation. In this brain which could viewed as the, *diencephalons* consisting of the two structures:

1. The *Thalamus*: processing information reaching the cerebral cortex from the rest of the central nervous system

2. The *Hypothalamus*: regulating autonomic, endocrine and visceral functions.

   7. The application layer is mostly responsible for the types of communication being processed. In the brain, it could be considered the *cerebral hemisphere*, which is responsible for future action, hearing, image and vision of information.

The layered diagram illustrates that, there exits a physical world, where daily events are triggered. In the daily events, our brain encounters humans, places, food, machines, computers and many more different events. In our human body, we have five kinds of senses: see, hear, touch, smell, taste, and feel. These senses are converted to images. Which are now, captured by short term memory (STM) in the brain which is called "Hippocampus". 0 or 1 number of occurrences of images will trigger STM. But when, there is more number of occurrences of the same images then these stored images will be passed to long term memory (LTM) which could be Neocortex in human brain. When there is more number of occurrences of images in LTM, it will result into behavior of human. The behavior could be divided into two types: Verbal and Non-verbal.

The Network OSI model is similar to the brain, but in more important ways it is not. As we saw, brain is organized to do any particular function based on the goal set by human emotions. Any new experiences are stored in form of images in our STM, with repetitive occurrence of the same event or experience results into long term storage. This long term storage is done in Neurocortex of the brain. The chapter concludes that human brain does not reflect the fact that it is exactly specific and similar to working of Network OSI model but as it can be seen that ants and bees do their learning collectively. The mind of swarm is sum of thousands upon thousands of simple decisions executed by individual members. The same approach is followed which showed that, individual organ of human brain makes individual decision for working of brain and driving behavior in humans

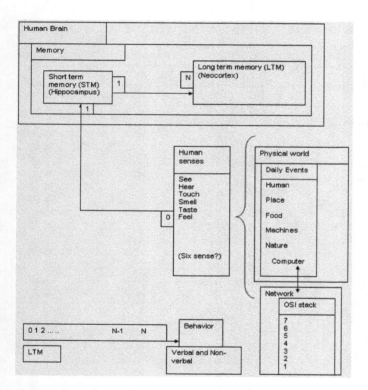

**Figure 9** The layered structure of the brain which could result into behavior.

Since the layered structure of the brain illustrated in the diagram shows how the behavior of the humans could be predicted. Henceforth, The CBOM diagram will predict the similarities between the OSI model and human brain. The Cognitive brain OSI model diagram is illustrated in the Appendix 3 section of the thesis for future references.

The aim of the Chapter was to give insights on Future of Communication Technology. The history of internet communication technology, and the trend towards the predicted cognitive networking or cognitive Internet, Cognitive internet (CI) is area of science will be inherently a multidisciplinary area of research. The principal purpose in CI will be to study human behavior on the Internet together with relevant research done previously in the field of behavioral science, cognitive science, psychological science and biological and Internet technology. Although, the topic of the Chapter falls into the categories of CI, much of the details on this topic are not covered. Only those topics are covered which are related to understanding the human behavior on the Internet.

Sociability is important as well as usability of applications in the Internet. While usability is concerned with making sure that the application, software and system is consistent, predictable, and easy and satisfying to use, sociability and the social aspect of building and maintaining an online community focuses on processes and styles of social aspect in interaction that support HBI to some extent.

There will always be an argument to model psychology with technology or technology with psychology however; combining psychology with technology will give rise to new technology called psycho technology. To understand the Internet technology in broader ways, interaction between human and the technology through the Human Computer Interaction becomes essential. BCI techniques are only studied in this thesis but these techniques are not used to model HBI.

The network OSI model thus looks somewhat similar to the workings of the human brain. When using the Internet, any patterns of behavior generated by humans are on top of Application Layer on the OSI model.

# 3  Methods, Design and Implementation

*The machine itself makes no demands and holds out no promises: it is the human spirit that makes demands and keeps promises. In order to re-conquer the machine and subdue it to human purposes, one must first understand it and assimilate it. So far we have embraced the machine without fully understanding it.*

—Lewis Mumford

The aim of this chapter is to draw an analysis from this phase together with Survey, Interviews and Observation. Various comparisons and study of methods together with the design is expected to give result, which will be further analyzed and evaluated to draw conclusion.

Three different types of method were used to test HBI. These methods were the surveys and Questionnaires; think aloud method and focus group. Based on the subjectivity, Objectivity, Quantitative and Qualitative methods human can be tested.

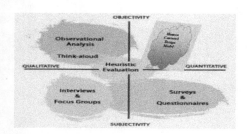

Figure 10: User centric model focusing on testing human behavior.

## 3.1 Observing and Coding Behavior.

*"Theory without Experiment is empty."*

*"Experiment without Theory is blind."*

—H. Pagels

The participants while doing the task show many types of behavior. Most of the times human may laugh, smile, drum their fingers on the table, shout, and look aimlessly around. These are all behavioral patterns which can be measured. The observation of the verbalization can be done but it may be difficult to note subtle or fleeting behavior. The unconscious behavior is difficult to predict for the participants. To measure such behavior it requires specialized equipment. For example Eye tracking system, Heart rate and Face recognition system. Such equipment can measure heart rate, pupil dilation, sweating and nervousness. There are many personal approaches to note the behavior. Tullis and Albert in their book entitled "Measuring the User experience" has demonstrated that, there are many different approaches to take notes during the usability test. Some is "stream-of-consciousness" approach where they narrate the events of the session; others use forms where they take specific notes on various events and behaviors pattern shown, and still others like data-logging tool that automatically records the entries. There is a division of the participant's overt behavior into two major general categories: verbal and nonverbal. Verbal behavior includes anything a participant says and Nonverbal behaviors include various activities that the participants actually do.

In verbal behavior useful information can be caught by observing participants emotional and mental state. Participants probably could make comments negative or positive. The verbal behavior can be categorized with following:

- Strongly positive comments (e. g., "This is terrific!")
- Other positive comments (e. g., "That was pretty good.")
- Strongly negative comments (e. g. "I don't much like the way that worked")
- Other negative comments(e. g., "It would have been better if ...")
- Questions (e. g., "How does this work?")
- Variation from expectation (e. g., "This isn't what I was expecting to get.")
- Stated confusion or lack of understanding (e. g., "This page doesn't make any sense.")
- Stated frustration (e. g., "At this point I'd just shut it off!")

In this research, "Usability Test Observation Coding Form" was used to measure verbal behavior. This form was used for each task that the participants attempts. This form was selected because it was believed that Subjects will show signs of verbal or non-verbal behavior and it would be easy to jot down these behaviors on this form. Sometimes the nonverbal behaviors may be frustrating or impatience on the part of humans.

- Frowning/Grimacing/Unhappy
- Smiling/Laughing/Happy
- Surprised/Unexpected
- Furrowed brow/Concentration
- Evidence of impatience
- Leaning in close to screen
- Variation from expectation
- Fidgeting in chair
- Random mouse movement
- Groaning/Deep sigh
- Rubbing head/eyes/neck

In non verbal behavior mostly facial expression such as smiling, looks of surprise, furrowing brow or showing body gestures such as leaning close to the screen, rubbing the head is shown by the participants. It is useful to record the frequency of non verbal behaviors. It is also useful to see how these behavior changes with the different designs or when comparing different tasks or products. Some of the behaviors discussed earlier were overt behavior which required an expert observer to observe and record them but there are other kinds of behavior which needs an equipment to capture. These are facial expression, eye-tracking, pupil diameter, skin conductance among others. One of the key to communication is recording face to face expression in human to human interaction. Tullis and Albert reports that many psychologists have argued facial expressions are more accurate. One can video records the expression and do a detailed analysis of an observer to get an overview of facial expression. Eye-tacking has been most common for testing humans. Many eye-tracking technologies use a combination of an infrared video camera and infrared light source to track where the participants are looking. The location of corneal reflection changes relative to pupil as the participants moves his or her eyes. Skin conductivity is measured using Galvanic Skin Responses (GSR), which measures the resistance. Heart rate is also associated with stress when the heart beat faster it is probably because of stress. There have been several studies to determine if skin conductivity and heart rate could be used as the indicators of stress or other adverse reactions in testing humans. Other several promising techniques are slowly rising to capture human behavior, such as mouse that registers how tightly it is being gripped.

One of the techniques used to capture and record the behavior of the human is by using observation techniques. Next chapter gives detail perspectives on these existing techniques of testing user centric behaviors.

## 3.2 Observational Analysis

*"Do not believe in anything simply because you have heard it. Do not believe in anything simply because it is spoken and rumored by many. Do not believe in anything simply because it is found written in your religious books. Do not believe in anything merely on the authority of your teachers and elders. Do not believe in traditions because they have been handed down for many generations. But after **observation and analysis**, when you find that anything agrees with reason and is conducive to the good and benefit of one and all, then accept it and live up to it."*

—Siddhartha Gautama

One of the natural methods of understanding the human is by observation. There are several techniques for the observation. The evaluator watches and records the human action either by means of observation where the human being observed is taking part in the process of being observed or by third party. In third party the evaluator observes and has no direct involvement in the task. It is viewed from the perspective of the human who inhabit the setting in confined environment. A clear focus of attention for the participants could be gathered. Observational analysis seeks to understand natural occurrence of the activities. There could be several techniques for the observation. The evaluator watches and records the human action which is very simple and can produce highly valid, accurate results. Important information may be lost which is further simplified by asking humans to describe their action during interaction. Such method of describing human action after the completion of the task is called "thinking aloud".

There could also be several methods to record the human action. One of the cheapest and sometimes difficult methods is "pen and pencil method". Another method could be audio recording which could be often more useful in "thinking aloud" techniques. Similarly, there is another method called video recording which has upper advantage of replaying the human actions more than once.

In addition to the observation techniques there exits several other methods such as "focus group", "think aloud" and "mental model" but all of these methods are not considered because of limitation in the research period.

## 3.3 Roadmap towards Building the Implementation Phase

The User study model or human study model is developed which will deploy and demonstrates the observation and quantitative method techniques in producing and gaining the result. The Question mark in the final box of human study model is kept for the prediction of an unknown.

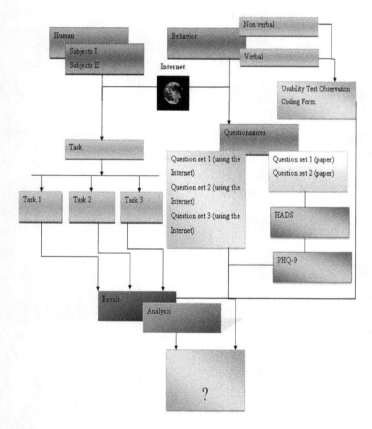

Figure 11: The human study model road map for building the implementation phase of HBI.

### 3.3.1 Web of Questions

The questionnaires is constructed English with the probabilities of worldwide distribution. An early version is being tested with seven human. Five different areas is being evaluated including social, usage, feelings, experience and a general area. All these are designed in such a way to collect understanding of HBI. The main research question is broken down into sub questions. Ten research sub-questions were formulated. These sub questions were-

1. How can the Internet be useful for meeting new people?
2. How long do you use the Internet?
3. What is the state of mind while using the Internet?
4. Do you lose track of time when using the Internet?
5. Number of addicted person known
6. Number of people who have felt anxiety or stress while on the Internet
7. Gender
8. Age
9. Occupation
10. Marital Status

The questions from 1-6 are research question dealing with understanding behavior of humans on the Internet whereas the sub-questions from 7-10 are demographics. To measure success, humans need to have specific goal or task in mind. The testing of humans while filling out questionnaire would generate into some behavior patterns such as they may laugh, shout, smile, groan, look aimlessly around the room, drum their fingers on the table, and fidget in their chair and so on. These behaviors are potentially measurable. The verbal behavior provides insight into a human's emotional and mental state while they are using a product. For example, "This is terrific!" strongly positive comment or "This website is terrible!" this is strongly negative comment. The nonverbal behaviors reveals about humans experience with product. For example, frowning, smiling, looks of surprise or body language like leaning close to screen, rubbing the head etc.

### 3.3.1.1 Number of Participants

A great debate has been going on for how much participants is needed to test human behavior and to measure user experiences. First time human who need an overview to understand what the ranges of services are? What is not available and what button select which actions. An intermittent user needs some familiar landmarks and safety during explorations. Frequent human demand shortcuts to speed the related task and extensive services to satisfy their varied needs. [76] There are two camps suggested by Tullis and Albert, those who believe that five participants are enough and those who believe five is nowhere near enough. It is said that 80% of the usability will be observed with first five participants [77]. It is also known as "magic number 5". One of the measure ways to figure out how many subjects are needed in the test is to find the probability of usability being detected by a single test participant. Some researchers do not agree on the number of participants being only five. [78] The recommendation by Tullis and Albert of "magic number 5" which works well under circumstances such as, scope of the evaluation should be limited and the human audience if well defined and well represented, is used.

### 3.3.1.2 Task Analysis.

In the task, Participants were asked to find the picture on the Internet with name "human behavior on the Internet_scope.jpg". It was assumed the task would be "Easy". The time allocated for the completion of item was 2 minutes. Similarly, Second item was given to download the picture "human behavior on the Internet_scope.jpg" in the system and upload it again with different name on the Internet. It was assumed the task would be "Difficult" and the time allocated for the item was 5 minutes. In addition, third item was given to visit the social networking web site such as (Face book, hi5, MySpace, Orkut, LinkedIn etc) and to create a profile (only one) with name "hbi_study". And, upload the picture "human behavior on the Internet_scope.jpg". It was assumed the task would be "Very Difficult" and the time allocated for the item was 7 minutes. The formats of the task being given to participants are appended in the Appendix 4 section of the thesis.

## 3.3.2 Detailed Internet Anxiety Questionnaire

A more detailed list of questionnaire was created which aimed at the measurement of Internet anxiety models shown in figure below. Subjects were asked total of nine questions. Internet anxiety was measured with the following items.

1. It is easy to use the Internet.
2. I cannot find what I am looking in the Internet.
3. I feel anxious when Internet is not working.
4. My anxiety about internet bothers me when I have to wait long for a web page to appear.
5. I know what the Internet is.
6. How much you have used the Internet?
7. I visit Face book, hi5, My Space, Orkut etc.
8. I am uncomfortable using the Internet
9. Best thing I like being in the Internet

It is assumed that, there are seven types of the Internet anxiety of using the Internet. First Four existing types of factors were developed by author. (Presno, 1998) remaining last three factors are discussed in this paper. The Internet anxiety types measured seven factors based on diagram drawn. These factors are:

[1]    Internet terminology anxiety

[2]    Internet search anxiety

[3]    Internet time delay anxiety

[4]    general fear of the Internet failure

[5]    Experience anxiety

[6]    Usage anxiety

[7]    Environment and attraction anxiety

The questions were answered using two, three, four and six point Likert-Scale consisting of statements on Internet that could be answered "yes" (entirely agree), "no" (entirely disagree). Internet terminology anxiety was referred to by an item such as "I know what is Internet". Internet search anxiety was referred to by an item such as "I cannot find what I am looking in Internet". Internet time delay anxiety was measured to by an item such as "I feel anxious when internet is not working" and "My anxiety about internet bothers me when I have to wait long for a web page to appear". General fear of Internet failure was measured to by an item such as "I feel anxious when Internet is not working". Experience anxiety was measured to by an item such as "I am uncomfortable using the Internet". Usage anxiety was measured by an item such as "how much you have used the Internet" and "Best thing I like being in Internet". Environment and attraction anxiety was measured to by an item such as "I visit Face book, hi5, MySpace, Orkut etc".

Figure 12: Overview on Seven types of Internet anxiety overview.

### 3.3.3 Internet Addiction Questionnaires

Internet Addiction is used to describe variety of behavior and problems using the Internet. Addiction can be inappropriate involvement in social networking sites, immoderate gaming, or even blogging, or internet shopping. "Internet addicts suffer from emotional problems such as depression and anxiety-related disorders and often use the fantasy world of the Internet to psychologically escape unpleasant feelings or stressful situations."[101] Internet usage can also become sometime addictive, following screening tool found on the center for online addiction, which was used to detect internet addiction. Two measures were taken to measure the Internet addiction test. In the first measure Participants were asked to fill up the 9 questions in the QS2 and in the second measure participants were asked to visit Internet addiction website to test Internet addiction Test (IAT) and fill up the questionnaire developed by Dr. Kimberly Young. In the first measure these were the questions in the QS2. Following questionnaires were separately given to each participant. These questionnaires were:

1. Do you think about previous online activity or anticipate your next online session?
2. Have you repeatedly made unsuccessful efforts to control, cut back, or stop the Internet use?
3. Do you feel restless, moody, depressed, or irritable when attempting to cut down or stop the Internet use?
4. Do you repeatedly stay online longer than originally intended?

5. Have you neglected sleep, proper diet, or exercise just to surf?
6. Have you experienced eyestrain or back strain because of your Internet use?
7. Have you jeopardized a significant relationship, job, or educational or career opportunities because of the Internet?
8. Have you lied to others to conceal the extent of your involvement with the Internet?
9. Do you use the Internet as a way of escaping from the problems or feelings of helplessness, guilt, anxiety, or depression?

The item 1 in the above questionnaire is the preoccupation with the Internet. When a human is thinking about Internet activities or anticipating of next on-line session. Repetition or and unsuccessful efforts to control, cut back or stop the use of the Internet is for the item 3. The Feelings of moodiness or depression or irritability or restlessness when attempting to slow down the use of the internet is given by item 3. With the increasing amount of time use of the internet is increasing to achieve satisfaction which reveals to the item 4. Not taking care of social activities like sleeping, exercise or proper diet simply to surf is taken care by item 5. Some humans might feel the eyestrain or back strain because of the Internet use which is given by item 6. Jeopardized or risked loss of significant relationship, job and educational or career opportunities because of the Internet is handled by item 7. Lies to therapists, family members or other to conceal the extent of involvement with the Internet is given by item 8 and lastly, the use of the Internet as the way to escape from the everyday problems or to relieve a feeling of hopelessness, guilt, anxiety, and depression is given by item 9. These entire questions give some signs of Internet addiction. Researchers suggest that answering yes to five or more questions probably means that the Internet is creating some kind of problems. The cutoff score is consistent with number of criteria such as pathological gambling.

There are many researchers such as, including Carol Potera and Jonathan Bishop, who agrees that Internet Addiction is inappropriately named.[79] The analogy is made to an environment: a person cannot be truly addicted to living in a favorite town no matter how distressing a change of home might be, and it follows the similar analogy that "goldfish cannot be addicted to living in a pond". There are several problems caused by Internet addiction which may result in personal, academic, financial and occupational hazards in real life. Those who are addicted to internet spend more time using the Internet and less time with the real human in their lives. There might be argument because of excessive use of the Internet. Some kind of financial problems might occur for the amount of time spent on-line and for the payment of service charges. Internet addicts come in many shapes and sizes. Human may some times pretend to be someone other than themselves using the Internet. The creation of anonymous life using the Internet might be suffering from fear, low self esteem and fear of disapproval from others.

## 3.4 Human Study Model Implementation

*"Discovery consists of seeing what everybody has seen and thinking what nobody has thought."*

—Albert Szent-Gyorgyi

The aim of the chapter is to draw an implementation model for capturing the HBI. The chapter also provides various methods and measure taken to implement behavior. Finally, data were collected through the screening process of numerous set of design of Questionnaires, implementation of models, survey and observation.

### 3.4.1 Implementation Model

The model being implemented to test the behaviors of the humans using the Internet has been developed. Two types of subject were being used. One subject was named as Subject I, another types of subjects were named as Subject II. Usability Test recording form was used for each participant. This form was used to record both the verbal and non-verbal behaviors of humans using the Internet. The task was chosen which was based on the Internet. The task contained three modules which were divided into task 1, task 2 and task 3 based on the level of difficulties.

These three different tasks were given three different times for completion of the task, and as for the level of difficulty of the task. One of the methods which were used to test the human behaviors together with the several methods was Questionnaires and Survey. The questions were divided into five different set. These questionnaires set were measured based on pen and paper and using the Internet. There were all together three set of questionnaires which were asked to be fulfilled using the Internet. Next set of questionnaires contained couple of them which was asked to be filled using the pen and paper methods. And, together with the questionnaires two additional set of questions were advised to be completed, these were HADS and PHQ-9. The set of questionnaires and the task was combined to measure behaviors of humans using the Internet. These behaviors were measured on following terms- anxiety, depression, addicted and stress of using the Internet.

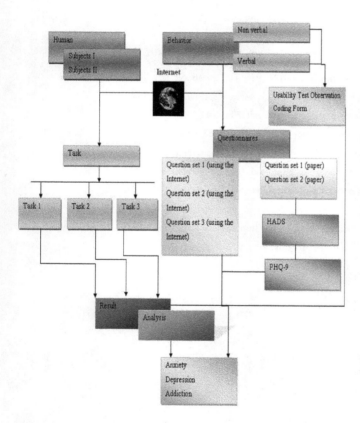

Figure 13: The human study model implemented to test behavior of humans using the Internet.

### 3.4.2 Metrics for Measuring Behavior

The Measure Scales used in the thesis are:

**3.4.2.1 The Internet Addiction Test (IAT; Young, 1998b)**: The measure consisted of 20 items for assessing and understanding behavior of humans with the Internet. Example of such item include: "How often do you neglect household chores to spend more time on-line?"; "How often do you form new relationships with fellow on-line human?"; "How often do you block out disturbing thoughts about your life with soothing thoughts of the Internet?" Higher the score, higher the problem faced with the Internet usage.

**3.4.2.2 Hospital Anxiety and Depression Scale (HADS; Zigmond & Snaith, 1983)**: The measure scale consisted of 14 items, 7 assessing depression and rest assessing anxiety. Example of such depression items includes: "I still enjoy the things I used to enjoy"; "I can laugh and see the funny side of things". Example of such anxiety item includes: "Worrying thoughts go through my mind"; "I get a sort of frightened feeling as if something awful is about to happen". The higher score represents higher level of anxiety and depression. It was chosen to measure negative behavior of humans with the Internet. It has been also widely used in clinical and non-clinical research. HADS shows the signs of good validity and reliability.

**3.4.2.3 Patent Health Questionnaires (PHQ-9; Spitzer R et al., 1999)**: The measure scale consisted of 9 items. Example of such items includes: "Feeling down, depressed, or hopeless"; "Feeling bad about yourself-or that you are a failure or have let yourself or your family down". The higher score represents higher level of problems faced over the last 2 weeks. It was chosen to measure behavioral feeling of the human.

### 3.4.3 Questionnaires for Testing Human Behaviors

There were all together five questionnaires set which were divided into two types. One was using the pen and paper and another was using the Internet. Following set and measure taken are given in details:

- **Questionnaires set 1 (QS1)**: This set consisted of nine items which was given to fill with pen and paper.
- **Questionnaires set 2 (QS2):** This set consisted of nine items which was also given to fill with pen and paper.
- **Questionnaires set 3 (QS3)**: This set consisted of 20 items questionnaires that measured mild, moderate and severe level of the Internet addiction. Participants were asked to visit the web page of these questionnaires using the Internet and record the score on the sheet of the paper provided to them.

- **Questionnaires set 4 (QS4)**: This set of questionnaires consisted of 10 items, participants were asked to visit the link using the Internet and fill up the questionnaires.
- **Questionnaires set 5 (QS5):** This set consisted of nine items which was given to fill with using the Internet. These questionnaires were exactly similar to the questionnaires set 1.

### 3.4.4 Task Measures

Three different tasks was given to humans, with level of difficulty defined as easy, difficult and very difficult for task 1, task 2 and task 3 respectively. To complete the Task 2, human were asked to complete the task 1 and similarly, to complete the task 3, human were asked to complete the task 2. These ways human will sequentially to go through the task.

- **Task 1 Measure**

One of the Quantitative method used to record the humans behavior for navigation through search engines and allow one to derive behavior metrics such as how many times certain browsing function is invoked or average length of browsing function was done using Markovian Modeling of User's cognitive behavior on the World Wide Web.

- **Task 2 Measure**

Humans Uploading and Downloading behavior was measured in this task. The task completion time was measured by allowing humans to download a picture from the Internet and again upload it back in the Internet.

- **Task 3 Measure**

Creation of the profile in social networking web pages (Face book, hi5, MySpace, Orkut, and LinkedIn) was final task given to humans. The measure for this task was assumed to be very difficult.

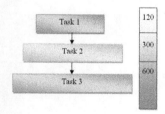

Figure 14: Task Measurement (Task1=120 seconds, Task 2=300 seconds and Task 3=600 seconds)

### 3.4.4.1 Task 1 Measure

In the task 1 measure, The Qualitative method used to capture the Internet activity of the participants was used carried out by Dr. George Meghabghab [4]. Let us suppose a search engine, which humans can perform the following functions:

a. Connect to the "Home page" of the search engine. The humans can loop over the home search engine.

b. Search the Internet for answers to the query after using the keyboard search, The human stage is in problem solving state, where they can loop over a search they have done.

c. Depending upon the set of results returned by search engine, user can set result returned by search engine, by evaluating result returned, which can constitute the scanning state. The state constitutes "shallow interpretations" of the set of results returned, which is part of the browse state. The state is part of the "browse" state and it constitutes a final step in knowledge filtering.

d. In the actual query, browse the link provided in resulting search. Human can loop over the web page that they have already browsed.

e. Selection of one of the links which was result of the search is done and viewing of additional information such as description, summary, ranking etc. This state is because of the consequences of the fact that human have goal in the mind, they are in final decision state which matches their knowledge state.

f. Backtrack to the previous screens if the link viewed does not contain the answer. It can be moving between different stages such as browse and select, or select and search or search and home.

g. Human should not wander on the web aimlessly when they are given a query. They have been given predefined task. The goal of the task 1 is to find the answer to the query. They either "succeed" or "fail" in the task. They can loop over the same web page, browse same link in the web but should not do it aimlessly.

The cognitive map is made based on these different stages which constitutes the framework for the study. State Si is used to represent a state at time i. One of the constraints human could go through is time and information constraints. Time constraint is time taken to answer a given query for the task 1 on the Internet. Information constraint is result of loads of information returned and refined search needed.

Human cannot have two constraints at the same given time; they are not supposed to query the web and browser at the same time. For any time i different than j, state Si, is different from State Sj, where i! = j: Si! =Sj

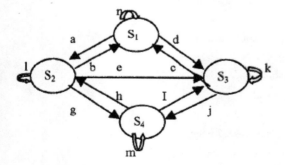

Figure 15: Markovian Modeling of User's Cognitive Map of the Web (S1=Home, S2=Browser, S3=Search, S4= Select). Total of five participants was selected in this study. The role of these participants was to fill the different values of the edges a, b, c, d, e, f, g, h, i, j, k, l, m, n which are in need. [4]

Participants were not given any details about the cognitive map so it was assumed that their behavior is not affected and the results will not be biased. The time spent on the task 1 helps in explaining the situation participants are going through. Any behavior which is not taken care for the figure 1 is recorded using the Usability Test Observation Coding form. The web engine selected was Google. Google search engine was selected because human will limit the time spent searching for information in different search engines. It was assumed that, the task 1 was very specific and no alternatives were offered to the participants. Results from the task 1 shows that human were able to perform the task at ease. Participants were asked to find an answer for the following question. Find the picture on the Internet with name "human behavior on the Internet_scope". The results showed that, human were able get success browsed more than they searched, and searched more than stayed Home. Those who failed the query most often they, searched than browsed and browsed than they selected web. The study cited Meghabghab gives results similar to those found in this study. [4]

### 3.4.4.2 Task 2 and Task 3 Measures

In the task 2 measures, The Qualitative method used to capture the Internet activity of the participants were used. Let us suppose following functions are performed by the humans for the completion of the task 2.

a.  For the accomplishment of the task 2, task 1 has to be carried out therefore, steps a, b, c, d, e, f, and g were necessary.

b.  In addition, User will first perform the task which for the following question. "Download the picture with name human behavior on the Internet_scope in the System and Upload it again with different name on the Internet.

In the task 3 measure, Let us suppose following functions were performed by the humans using the Internet.

a.  Connect to the "Home page" of the Social Networking web sites. These web sites could be based on the personal choice of the human. For example face book, hi5, MySpace, Orkut, LinkedIn etc.

b.  Sign up for the Web site, in these web sites Human are asked to fill out the forms with personal information such as Full name, Date of Birth and Email address etc.

c.  To be successful in the task 3, human must complete the steps mentioned in the task 1 and task 2 respectively.

The results showed that, human were able get success in downloading and uploading of the picture very easily.

### 3.4.4.3 Task Result

The overall task completion times for five participants are shown in the table below. The result from the task shows that all the participants were capable of performing the task within the given time for each task.

Table 2: Task with the overall time taken by participants to complete each task and total time taken for the completion of the entire tasks.

| Participants Id | Task 1 | Task 2 | Task 3 | Total time taken |
|---|---|---|---|---|
| 1 | 10 | 20 | 30 | 60 |
| 2 | 30 | 40 | 50 | 120 |
| 3 | 10 | 25 | 55 | 90 |
| 4 | 120 | 60 | 300 | 480 |
| 5 | 15 | 20 | 25 | 60 |
| Note: Task Time is expressed in seconds. | | | | |

These result from the table showed that two participants took more than 100 seconds of the time to complete the overall task. Except that, three participants completed the task in less than 100 seconds. As the value set for the task 1 was 120 seconds, all the participants were able to complete the task within the allowed time frame. Majority of the participants completed the task 1 within 20 seconds of the time. For the task 2, the time taken by the participants to complete the task 2 was very less. Majority of the participants completed the task 2 within 50 seconds of the time. Similarly, for the task 3, Majority of the participants completed the task 3 within 70 seconds of the time. From the above data, only one participant took a bit longer time to complete not only the first task but all of the tasks. Only Task Calculation is not sufficient to measure the behaviors of the human using the Internet. Therefore, a new method was developed to manipulate and observe behaviors. This method uses the Questionnaires to measure the behaviors and is known as Simple Questionnaires methods.

## Summary

The aim of the Chapter was to model human centered design and implement the model based on user study model developed in the study. There are various methods for usability studies Such as Qualitative and Quantitative methods. The user study model developed in the study covers these two methods. Task was given to the participants who were divided into three smaller sub tasks with the level of difficulty. These tasks were given for specific period of the time. Time on the task was measured with average, median, geometric mean and confidence intervals.

User study model developed uses both Qualitative and Quantitative methods. The qualitative method is used through Interviews, Focus groups and Observational analysis. Task calculation was performed through this approach whereas; Quantitative method is used through Survey and Questionnaires. Online Questionnaires and Offline Questionnaires were distributed using this approach. Both the method studied provides better results.

In addition, two types of questionnaire set were constructed to understand anxiety, addiction of using the Internet. Furthermore, online survey from the center of net addiction was also used to understand behavior of humans. Many different measures such as IAT, HADS, SQM and Markovian Method were explained. By using the qualitative method such as Observational analysis, think-aloud, interviews and document analysis and quantitative method of task analysis the expected more precise result are expected. These measures are the key to calculate the result. The result obtained in this chapter together with the methods will be further be analyzed in the chapter analysis. The task calculation showed that, Majority of the participants completed the three different tasks in the given time frame.

# 4. Human Analysis and Evaluation

*"It requires a very unusual mind to undertake the **analysis** of the obvious."*

—Alfred North Whitehead

The purpose of the chapter is to analyze numerous data's and information collected for capturing the HBI. The chapter demonstrates the diagrams and compares the result on various methods and measure taken to implement human behavior.

## 4.1 Analysis of the Questionnaires

The questionnaires analysis is done based on pen and paper, observation and on the Internet. The user study model which was implemented for the questionnaires is shown below in the diagram. Only the small portion of the diagram is illustrated for simplicity. The questionnaires were divided into two major categories. One category was using the Internet and another category was using the pen-paper method. Three question sets were divided such as Question set1, Question set2 and Question set3 which were answered by the participants using the Internet. Similarly, two set of questions were divided using the pen-paper method which were Question set1 and Question set2 respectively.

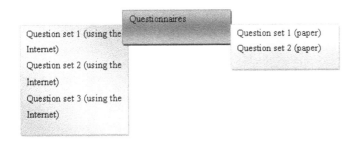

Figure 16: Small portion of user study diagram which illustrates the questionnaires and there types.

## 4.1.1 Using the Internet

In the first stage, Twenty Participants responded to the items in which total of 17 participants answered the QS1, using the Internet. In the second stage, Fifty Five participants responded to the items in which total of 52 answered the QS1, using the Internet. The QS1 using the internet consisted of nine items. The question set 2 using the internet was similar to the Question set 1 of the pen and paper. There was no difference recorded when the participants answered the questionnaires using the pen and paper or using the Internet while answering Question set 2.

In Question set 1, questions were most general types; these types of question were selected simply for broader range of the audience. The result of this short survey concludes that majority of the participants showed the seven types of anxiety while using the Internet. The graph and other relevant data are shown in the appendix 5 of this thesis.

In Question set 3, using the internet consisted of twenty items. The center for online addiction web pages were used to measure the score for IAT. Following responses were recorded from the two types of the participants: Subject I and Subject II.

Table 3: Five participants answered the questionnaires. The detailed responses from the participants are shown below.

| Participants Id | Questionnaire set 3 | Participants Id | Questionnaire set 3 |
|---|---|---|---|
| | Score (IAT) | | Score (IAT) |
| 1 | 50 | 1 | 61 |
| 2 | 41 | 2 | 39 |
| 3 | 62 | 3 | 52 |
| 4 | 48 | 4 | 48 |
| 5 | 36 | 5 | 27 |

The IAT measure was adapted from the center of online addictions and based on that, evaluation of the subjects were done. The higher you're score, the greater you're level of addiction and the problems your Internet usage causes. Here's a general scale to help measure your score:

1. **20 - 49 points:** You are an average on-line user. You may surf the Web a bit too long at times, but you have control over your usage.

2. **50 -79 points:** You are experiencing occasional or frequent problems because of the Internet. You should consider their full affect on your life.

3. **80 - 100 points:** Your Internet usage is causing significant problems in your life. You should evaluate the affect of the Internet on your life and address the problems directly caused by your Internet usage.

Based on the above table, the IAT was recorded for the participants in two different categories: Subject I and Subject II. The table above on the left shows two human experiencing occasional or frequent problems because of the Internet usage. Similarly, from the table 4 on the right, two different humans were experiencing the occasion or frequent problem of the Internet. The above data were recorded using the questionnaires developed by Dr. Kimberly Yong. Center of online addiction uses set of 20 questions to calculate the above measured response from the humans.

## 4.1.2 Using Pen and Paper

The **QS1** using the pen and paper consisted of nine items. The detailed responses from the participants are similar to the QS1 using the Internet; Rest of the data was omitted for the simplicity. More detailed justification is done in Evaluation section in the next chapter. One of the responses is shown below: The **QS2** using the pen and paper consisted of nine items. The detailed responses from the participants are shown below:

Table 4: Participant response is shown below.

| Participants Id | Questionnaire set 2 | | HADS | | PHQ-9 |
|---|---|---|---|---|---|
| | Yes | No | Anxiety | Depression | |
| 1 | 6 | 3 | 5 | 2 | 1 |
| 2 | 6 | 3 | 13 | 5 | 11 |
| 3 | 7 | 2 | - | - | - |
| 4 | 6 | 3 | 10 | 3 | 3 |
| 5 | 5 | 4 | 6 | 6 | 7 |

In the QS 2, Researchers suggest that answering yes to five or more questions probably means that the Internet is creating some kind of problems. The cutoff score is consistent with number of criteria such as pathological gambling. It was found that, all the participants said "yes" to five or more items from the questionnaire set 2, which indicate problematic Internet Usage. In the HADS, The grading is done on the scale of 0 - 7 = Non-case 8 – 10 = Borderline case 11+ = Case. Only four of the participants answered these questionnaires for HADS and majority of them was recorded with Non-case or Borderline case. Only one participant seemed to have a Case. Similarly, PHQ-9 was used where only one participant had higher score of the depression scale.

## 4.2 Task Analysis

The task analysis was carried out by breaking down the entire task into three sub-tasks. The data was recorded for the five participants in Subject I category and another five participants in Subject II category. The total time taken is shown in the seconds. All the sub-tasks were analyzed with the graph being shown below. The table below shows the total time taken and the task completion rate in seconds for the Subject I.

In the task 1, with 95% CI, The Use the low and high values as the confidence intervals for the task times have been shown. These values correspond to the green-dashed lines in the graphs. They are the boundaries of the confidence interval. For example, the data entered from the table above for the task 1 times were: 10,30,10,120,15 (in any order) with a 95% confidence level, following is reported:

- Average Time: 22 seconds, 95% CI (6.1, 81.2)

The arithmetic mean is provided as a point of reference. The point to notice here is how the geometric mean is lower than the arithmetic mean; this is a symptom of a positively skewed distribution. The task 1 was analyzed which gave the following graph.

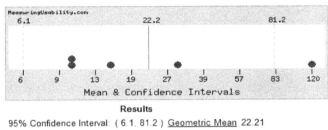

| 6.1 | 22.2 | 81.2 |

| 6 | 9 | 13 | 19 | 27 | 39 | 57 | 83 | 120 |

Mean & Confidence Intervals

**Results**

95% Confidence Interval: ( 6.1, 81.2 ) <u>Geometric Mean</u> 22.21

<u>Median</u>: 15

Arithmetic Mean     37     Observations   5

Arithmetic StDev     47.12

Figure 17: Task 1 measurement and analysis. [5]

In the task 2, with 95% CI, The Use the low and high values as the confidence intervals for the task times have been shown. These values correspond to the green-dashed lines in the graphs. They are the boundaries of the confidence interval. For example, the data entered from the table above for the task 2 times were: 20, 40, 25, 60, and 20 (in any order) with a 95% confidence level, following is reported:

- Average Time: 29 seconds, 95% CI (16.5, 54.4)

The arithmetic mean is provided as a point of reference. The point to notice here is how the geometric mean is lower than the arithmetic mean; this is a symptom of a positively skewed distribution The task 2 was analyzed which gave the following graph.

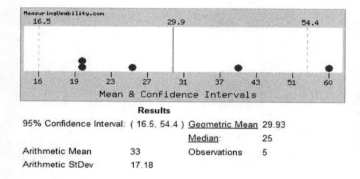

Figure 18: Task 2 measurement and analysis.[5]

In the task 3, with 95% CI, The Use the low and high values as the confidence intervals for the task times have been shown. These values correspond to the green-dashed lines in the graphs. They are the boundaries of the confidence interval. For example, the data entered from the table above for the task 3 times were: 30,50,55,300,25 (in any order) with a 95% confidence level, following is reported:

- Average Time: 57 seconds, 95% CI (16.9, 194.4)

The arithmetic mean is provided as a point of reference. The point to notice here is how the geometric mean is lower than the arithmetic mean; this is a symptom of a positively skewed distribution. The task 3 was analyzed which gave the following graph.

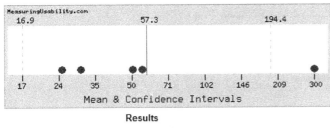

**Results**

95% Confidence Interval: ( 16.9. 194.4 ) <u>Geometric Mean</u> 57.32

<u>Median</u>: 50

Arithmetic Mean 92 Observations 5

Arithmetic StDev 116.97

Figure 19: Task 3 measurement and analysis. [5]

If we tested undefined human, assuming 0 passed and 5 failed the task, we would have an observed completion rate of 0% and we can be 95% confident the actual completion rate of the whole population is at least 0%. Similarly, If 0 humans fail the task, and 5 passed and 0 failed the task we can be 95% confident the actual completion is above 60%. In general, the task completion rate is above 60% which signifies that, more than 60% of the entire population of the student can perform the task in the context of the university.

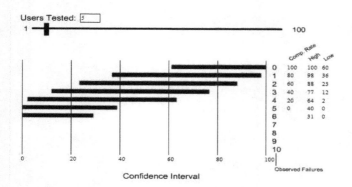

Figure 20: Confidence Interval testing with actual completion rate is above 60%. [5]

Similarly, the table for the total time taken and the task completion rate in seconds for the Subject II category is omitted. The average time recorded for the task completion in Subject II categories are: 20, 32 and 63 seconds, 95 % CI. By comparing these two task completion rate for two subjects it could be noted that, both the subject were able to finish the task successfully within the given time frame.

Now, let us calculate the CI for the binary task completion data. Why do we need to calculate CI for task completion data? We need to calculate CI because we are trying to make inference about the entire population of students and their task behavior on the Internet. The table below shows number of task carried out by each of the participants and number of successful task performed. The z-score represents a 95% CI or 95% of which are under normal curve equals 1.96 standard deviation above the mean 0. The proportion of successes is recorded. The "p" and "n" are adjusted which determines total number of trials and proportion of trails that were successes.

Table 5: The calculation of a confidence interval for binary task completion data with total number of task being calculated and number of successful task being carried out is shown below in the table.

| Calculation of a confidence interval for binary task completion data | |
|---|---|
| Total number of tasks: | 3 |
| Number of successful tasks: | 3 |
| Desired Confidence Level (normally 95%): | 95% |
| Calculations are then done below: | |
| z value for Confidence interval: | 1.960 |
| Proportion of successes: | 1.000 |
| p-adjusted: | 0.719 |
| n-adjusted: | 6.841 |
| Confidence Interval: | 0.337 |
| Lower Limit: | 38.3% |
| Upper Limit: | 105.6% |

The formula for calculating the Adjusted Wald confidence interval is as follows:

$$p_{adj} \pm z * \text{sqrt}(p_{adj}(1 - p_{adj})/n_{adj})$$

Where:

n = total number of trials

p = proportion of trials that were successes

z = the z-value corresponding to the desired confidence level

$p_{adj} = (n*p + z^2/2)/(n + z^2)$

$n_{adj} = n + z^2$

According to Sauro and Lewis [104] demonstrated that the Adjusted Wald Method of calculating a confidence interval works well for many of the situations we encounter in usability testing. The basic idea behind the Adjusted Wald Method [105] is that you need to adjust the observed proportion of task successes to take into account the small sample sizes commonly used in usability tests.

## 4. 3 Behavior and Subject Analysis

The usability test observation coding form was used which was helpful for determining two types of the behaviors of the participants: Verbal and Non-verbal. Most of the participants showed both the types of the behavior while using the Internet. These types of the behavior patterns are common in the narrowly selected group of the participants in the analysis for the case. These types of behavioral analysis for each of the participants are shown in appendix 2. The subject was categorized especially in two major areas. Subject I and Subject II. The subject I were, Participants (N=5) selected consisting of University students Mean average age of 25 years, all of them male. In the subject II categories, Participants (N=5) selected consisting of any other human being without the background of computer science. In the online questionnaires subject were not given any categories. These humans were mainly friends and those who were interested to participate for the online survey.

## 4.4 Internet Anxiety

Four types of Internet anxiety was identified by Presno by using qualitative study method. [80] These are: *Internet terminology anxiety*: anxiety produced by an introduction to a host of new vocabulary words and acronyms. *Net search anxiety*: anxiety produced by searching for information in a maze-like cyberspace. *Internet time delay anxiety*: anxiety produced by busy signals, time delays, and more and more people clogging the Internet. *General fear of Internet failure*: a generalized anxiety produced by fear that one will be unable to negotiate the Internet, or complete required work on the Internet. Additional three areas of the Internet anxiety from the qualitative study are constructed in this thesis. *Experience anxiety*: an anxiety produced by lack of concentration or focus. *Usage anxiety*: a generalized anxiety produced by excessive usage of the Internet. *Environment and attraction anxiety*: anxiety produced by content on the Internet. For example: interactive game, pornography, larger number of colorful applications etc. By using the Observation method, from the table below, it could be concluded that seven types of anxiety were determined from the humans. As there were two types of Subject in the study: Subject I and Subject II, Three participants felt more than five types of anxiety from the table below on the left. Whereas, five types of anxiety were observed from the table below on the right.

Table 6: Types of Anxiety recorded for Subject I and Subject II.

| Types of anxiety | p1 | p2 | p3 | p4 | p5 | p1 | p2 | p3 | p4 | p5 |
|---|---|---|---|---|---|---|---|---|---|---|
| Terminology | x | | x | | x | x | x | | x | x |
| Search | | x | x | x | | | x | x | x | x |
| Time delay | x | x | x | x | | x | | x | x | |
| general fear | | x | x | | | | x | x | | x |
| experience | x | | x | | x | x | | x | | x |
| Usage | x | x | | | x | x | x | | | x |
| Environment and attraction | x | x | x | x | x | x | x | | x | |

# Summary

The analysis was carried out with the help of User study model being implemented. The Questions were analyzed with the help of different types of questionnaires being constructed. Intentionally, Participants were given very general types of question to answer. Two types of Questionnaires were used: Using the Internet and Using the Pen and Paper method.

Task calculation was carried out by dividing the task into sub-task. Two types of subject were categorized based on skill level (novice, intermediate and expert human): Subject I and Subject II. It was found from the task analysis that humans using the Internet took less than a second to complete all of these tasks. Overall, calculation of the confidence interval was found above 60%. The literature studies of behaviors were proved qualitatively by analyzing the humans and recording their behavior using the usability test observation coding form.

In the Questionnaires using the pen and paper method, one of the natural methods of understanding the human is by observation was used. There are several techniques for the observation. It was evaluated by watching and recording the human action either by means of observation where the human being observed or also by taking part in the process of being observed.

Two schools of thought have emerged which confirms with the hypothesis that, there are two types of the behavior while using the Internet: Verbal and Non-Verbal behavior. In more general terms human using the Internet can use the content available on the Internet in two different ways: Positive or Negative. The gestures or types of human behavior shown could lead to anxiety.

# 5. Conclusions

*"There are three kinds of lies: lies, damned lies, and statistics."*

—Mark Twain

The result concludes that, human shows the increased anxiety level when using the Internet. In reference to above cited chapters, finding behaviors of the humans was carried out; these behaviors were distinguished in two types' verbal behaviors and non-verbal behaviors. The role of the content is very important in placing the behavior.

Human analysis and evaluation showed that, there are seven types of anxiety found on the Internet. Subject participants in this task took less than a second to complete the given task on the Internet. Since two types of subject samples were involved in the study: Subject I with computer background and Subject II without computer background. Subject I was tested first and then Subject II samples. By using Qualitative and Quantitative methods, it was recorded that, there were no differences between these two subject categories. With reference to above tables, it was found that, the entire three tasks were successfully carried out by participants within the given time frame. There are approximately 5,500 students in the university. [81] Subject I was tested with total number of task equals to 3, total number of successful task was recorded as 3. The Proportion of successes was recorded as 1.000. Therefore, out of 5,500 students in the university, 60% or above of them will likely be able to complete the given task on the Internet. Similarly, when Subject II samples were tested, it was found that, entire three tasks were successfully performed by the participants within the given time frame. Therefore, Out of 5,500 students in the university, 60% to 100% of them will likely be able to complete the task. In addition, with both the cases seven major types of anxiety were discovered in the participants. This shows that, humans can be 95% confident of performing the task on the Internet with likelihood of completing the task lies above 60%. The impact of the result is global which could be clearly stated that, either the student has computer background or not, they can easily use the any given task on the Internet with ease. In addition, two samples of anxiety measured also determines that, in this particular case-there were seven types of anxiety observed. The result is probably due to the fact that, in this particular case the participants were young adults of around with means age of 25 years.

## 5.1. Discussion

Taking the results and discussion into account, it appears to the authors knowledge that, "Internet has lulled humans with the sense of dependency to greater extent". Five types of hypothetical questions were answered in this study. These questions were: Do users shows increased or reduced anxiety level when using the Internet? What kinds of behaviors are shown when using the Internet? What is the role of the content? Finding types of the anxiety behaviors? And, How human process information at the internet interface?

Seven major types of anxiety were studied and validated: Internet terminology anxiety, Internet search anxiety, Internet time delay anxiety, and general fear of Internet failure anxiety, experience anxiety, usage anxiety, and environment and attraction anxiety. Two types of behavior (verbal and non-verbal) were formulated from relevant literature study, empirical analysis and evaluation. The study of Brain Computer Interface concludes that signal could be send in human brain physically to control and observe behavior of humans, however the BCI techniques were not used in the study and without using BCI techniques, the study conducted discovered sample of humans showing increased level of anxiety when using the Internet. The task completion behaviors of humans were calculated. It appears that, Out of 5,500 students in the university, 60% or above of them will be likely to complete the given task on the Internet.

With reference to task completion behavior, study concludes that, since the task performance behaviors of humans using the Internet was above 60%, any given task is easy to perform on the Internet. These tasks could be uploading the content, downloading the content, viewing the content and creating the profile in the social web pages such as Face book, LinkedIn, MySpace among others.

In addition, introductory study on CI and comparisons of human brain with OSI model was carried out in this thesis. Since till date, there is no relevant theory on human brain, development of how human brain triggers behavior could be useful to understand technology in future.

The goal of the study was to determine "how can we address the challenges such as Internet addiction, psychology and human computer interaction it is currently facing now?" In order to evaluate the main research question, the main research question was broken down into hypothesis. There were five different hypothesis formulated in the beginning of the research. Now, Let us try to discuss these hypotheses to see our method, design, evaluation and analysis of the research was supported (fully supported, partially supported and not supported) or not.

H1: *Do users shows increased or reduced anxiety level when using the Internet?*

Hypothesis 1 was fully supported. Human shows the sign of increased level of anxiety when using the Internet. It appears that, with any given task on the Internet number of anxiety increase in human. More number of participants said "yes" to five or more items from the QS 2, which indicates problematic Internet Usage.

Using HADS and PHQ-9 it was observed that, one participant seemed to have a Case of higher depression scale. Therefore, in this particular case users showed increased anxiety level when using the Internet.

H2: *What kinds of behaviors are shown when using the Internet?*

Hypothesis 2 was fully supported. Literature review revealed that there are two types of behavior shown by human using the Internet: Verbal and Non verbal. During Observation of behavior for the participants, Most of the times humans were laughing, smiling, drumming their fingers on the table and looking aimlessly around. These behaviors pattern was verbal and non-verbal. These types of the behavior patterns were observed among narrowly selected group of the participants.

H3: *What is the role of the content?*

Hypothesis 3 was partially supported. Role of content could determine the predicted or unpredicted human behavior on the Internet. Such as addiction, anxiety and stress of using the Internet, since humans were successfully able to complete the task with ease, it could be predicted that-any sort of given task for humans is very easy to do on the Internet. Therefore, the role of content has principal impact on how human behaves on the Internet.

H4: *Finding types of the anxiety behaviors?*

Hypothesis 4 was fully supported. It was found that in this particular case there are seven main area of anxiety in the humans: Internet terminology anxiety, Internet search anxiety, Internet time delay anxiety, general fear of Internet failure anxiety, experience anxiety, usage anxiety, and environment and attraction anxiety. Using Observation methodology and Comparing two types of subjects: Subject I and Subject II from the above tabular data, it concludes that- all the participants showed these above cited anxiety.

H5: *How human process information at the internet interface?*

Hypothesis 5 was partially supported. When human interacts with the internet interface, it appears that, everything that human senses such as sight, hearing, touch, smell and taste are processed as the information in the mind. This information could result in behavior such as verbal and non-verbal. Even if behavior initially disappears, it may partially return as undamaged parts of the brain reorganize their linkages. The human behavior in totality of processing information includes internal cognitive processes which can result in observable behavior. Processing of the information at the internet interface has the realistic approach such as thinking of mental processes as several railroad lines that all feed to same terminal [50, 53].

By the end of this discussion session, We can reach to the conclusion that, to reduce Internet anxiety, addiction and depression scale on the Internet, it is important to have many multicultural experiences, and control over own self behavior to accumulate successful experiences of behavior. The small sample size severely limits the applicability and generalization. Future studies should examine these complicated results to offer sufficient explanation and generalization.

## 5.2. Future Work

*"The state of mind which enables a man to do work of this kind is akin to that of the religious worshipper or the lover; the daily effort comes from no deliberate intention or program but straight from the heart."*

—Albert Einstein

From the book by Sir Tony Hoare, The first passage in *Communicating Sequential Processes* reads, "Forget for a while about computers and computer programming, and think instead about objects in the world around us, which act and interact with us and with each other in accordance with some characteristic pattern of behavior". The same idea is followed in the study of HBI.

- Large sample size, different demography structure and discovery of perfect user study model are needed, for larger impact and generalization.
- In contrast to several findings of negative effect in the Internet addiction, anxiety and depression group, some positive effects could be determined in future, building the framework for future learning Imagination, Investigation and Innovation..
- In depth analysis and comparisons of the human brain and the network open System Interconnection (OSI) model could be performed.

- The forms of anxiety identified suggest areas for future Internet development and research.
- Internet technology which can think on its own, "Cognitive Internet (CI)" could be invented in near future.

Despite the above limitations, undoubtedly the Internet has provided a collection of applications that is having a profound effect on mankind. Like the wheel, the plow, and steam power before it, it is a proving a truly differentiating tool in our world, changing the very ways in which we interact with each other. "The journey of thousand miles starts with the single step". Similarly, the evolution of new forms of socialization on Internet starts with HBI for providing new inventions to benefit society in the future.

## Bibliography and References

[1] ISC.org. Millions of host on the internet. *2008*Available: https://www.isc.org/

[2] Central Intelligence Agency. The DigiWorld in the global economy. *DigiWorld 2008*Available: https://www.cia.gov/library/publications/the-world-factbook/geos/xx.html; https://www.cia.gov/library/publications/the-world-factbook/fields/2184.html

[3] BCI-info. BCI scheme. *2008*Available: http://www.bci-info.tugraz.at/Research_Info/images/bci_scheme

[4] G. Meghabghab, "Fuzzy cognitive state map vs markovian modeling of user's web behavior," *Systems, Man, and Cybernetics, 2001 IEEE International Conference on,* vol. 2, pp. 1167-1172 vol.2, 2001.

[5] Sauro. J. *2008*Available: http://www.measuringusability.com/index.php

[6] Tim Berner's Lee. (2008, On WWW. *(June),* Available: http://www.sciencemag.org/cgi/content/full/313/5788/769

[7] DARPA. Internet information. *2008*Available: http://www.darpa.mil/body/arpa_darpa.html

[8] Internet Society. About internet technology. Available: http://www.isoc.org/

[9] W3C Semantic Web. (2008, Web consotorium. Available: http://www.w3.org/2001/sw/SW-FAQ

[10] Tim Berners-Lee, James Hendler and Ora Lassila. (2008, Available: http://www.sciam.com/article.cfm?id=the-semantic-web&print=true

[11] Simonson, Maurer, M. Torardi and Whitaker, "Development of a standardized test of computer literacy and a computer anxiety index," vol. 3, pp. 231-247, 1987.

[12] Robert E. Kraut. *2008*Available: http://www.cs.cmu.edu/~kraut/RKraut.site.files/articles/Bessiere06-Internet-SocialResource-DepressionL.pdf

[13] C. Chou. (2003, Incidence and correlates of internet anxiety among high school teachers in taiwan. *Computers in Human Behaviour 19*pp. 731-749.

[14] B. F. SKINNER. *2008*Available: http://www.bfskinner.org/aboutfoundation.html;http://www.bfskinner.org/f/Science_and_Human_Behavior.pdf

[15] L. Baumeister Cohen and Wills. (2008, Available: http://books.nap.edu/openbook.php?record_id=10002&page=73

[16] D. Norman. *2008*Available: http://www.hci-journal.com/editorial/si-beauty-intro.pdf

[17] S. K. Kalwar, "Human behavior on the internet," *Potentials, IEEE*, vol. 27, pp. 31-33, 2008.

[18] David Lochhead. *2008*Available: http://works.bepress.com/cgi/viewcontent.cgi?article=1009&context=david_lochhead

[19] ISOC.org. *2008*Available: http://www.isoc.org/internet/history/brief.shtml

[20] Eklundh, K. S., Groth, K., Hedman, A., Lantz, A., Rodriguez, H. & Sallnas, E., "The world wide Web as a social infrastructure for knowledge-oriented work," *Cognition in a Digital World*, pp. 97-126, 2003.

[21] Lazar, J., Preece, J, "Social Considerations in Online Communities: Usability, Sociability, and Success Factors. In:Oostendorp, H.v. (ed.)," *Cognition in a Digital World*, pp. 127-151, 2003.

[22] John Markoff. New york times news. *2008*Available: http://www.livinginternet.com/i/ii_roberts.htm; http://www.nytimes.com/2008/07/30/technology/30flaw.html?ref=technology

[23] Senator Martin J. Golden. Protecting children in the internet age. *2008*Available: http://www.senate.state.ny.us/sws/Protecting%20Children%20in%20the%20Internet%20Age.pdf

[24] Wellman, B and Boase, J and Chen, W., "The Networked Nature of Community:Online and Offline," *IT and Society*, vol. 1, 2002.

[25] Malcolm Owen Slavin and Daniel Kriegman, *the Adaptive Design of the Human Psyche: Psychoanalysis, Evolutionary Biology, and the Therapeutic Process.*. Fundar Editorial, September 25, 1992,

[26] D. Boyd. Friendster lost steam. is MySpace just a fad? *2008*

[27] Last, D. A., O' Donnell, A. M., & Kelly, A. E., "The effects of prior knowledge and goal strength on the use of hypertext." *Journal of Educational Multimedia and Hypermedia*, vol. 10, pp. 3-25, 2001.

[28] Kim, K. S., & Allen, B., "Cognitive and task influences on Web searching behavior." *Journal of the American Soceity for Information Science,* vol. 52, pp. 109-119, 2002.

[29] W. Yuan, "End-user searching behavior in information retrieval: A longitudinal study." *Journal of the American Soceity for Information Science,* vol. 48, pp. 227-229, 1997.

[30] Holscher, C., & Strube, G., "Web Search behavior of Internet experts and newbies." *Computer Networks,* vol. 33, pp. 337-346, 2000.

[31] AMA (American Medical Association). (2007, Online game addiction. Available:
http://articles.latimes.com/2007/jun/25/business/fi-games25

[32] Marny R. Hauge, Douglas A. Gentile and Berkeley Parents Network, "Game addicts," vol. 2008,

[33] Cause and Impact of Video Game addiction. Video game addiction. Available:
http://www.ndri.com/article/cause_and_impact_of_video_games_addiction_-211.html

[34] Philippe Naughton and Mark Griffiths. Online game addiction. Available:
http://www.timesonline.co.uk/tol/news/world/article553840.ece;
http://news.bbc.co.uk/2/hi/technology/4137782.stm

[35] Ian Williams. Online game addiction. Available:
http://www.vnunet.com/vnunet/news/2184523/online-addict-games-himself

[36] Martin F. Downs. Pornography addiction. Available:
http://men.webmd.com/guide/is-pornography-addictive

[37] A. Cooper and Putnam, Dana E., Planchon, Lynn A., & Boies,
Sylvain C., "Online Sexual Compulsivity: Getting Tangled in the Net."
*Sexual Addiction & Compulsivity: The Journal of Treatment and Prevention Page.*,
pp. 79-104,

[38] D. L. Delmonico, "Cybersex: High Tech Sex Addiction," *Sexual
Addiction & Compulsivity: The Journal of Treatment and Prevention Page.*, pp.
159-167,

[39] AAMFT Consumer Update. Sexual addiction. Available:
http://www.aamft.org/families/Consumer_Updates/Sexual%20Addicti
on.asp

[40] Healthy Minds. Content control. Available:
http://www.healthyminds.com/filters.pdf

[41] Videojug.com. Facebook addiction. *2008(May 15),* Available:
http://www.videojug.com/film/what-is-facebook-addiction

[42] Cat DiStasio. Social networking sparks antisocial behavior.
*2008* Available:
http://media.www.uwtledger.com/media/storage/paper642/news/2008
/04/24/ArtsEntertainment/Social.Networking.Sparks.Antisocial.Behavi
or-3350948-page2.shtml

[43] S. Kierkegaard, "Blogs, lies and the doocing: The next hotbed of
litigation?" *Computer Law & Security Report,*

[44] CNN.com. (October 22, 2006, Blogging news. *CNN* Available:
http://www.cnn.com/2006/WORLD/africa/10/22/sudan.darfur.un/in

dex.html;

http://news.bbc.co.uk/2/hi/africa/6076022.stm;http://www.nytimes.co
m/2007/12/06/business/06dyslexia.html?_r=1&oref=slogin

[45] E. Dickson. *2008*Available:
http://www.emilydickinsoninternationalsociety.org/

[46] Douglas R. Hofstadter, *Gödel, Escher, Bach: An Eternal Golden Braid.*
February 4, 1999, pp. 832.

[47] S. P. Levine, J. E. Huggins, S. L. BeMent, R. K. Kushwaha, L. A.
Schuh, M. M. Rohde, E. A. Passaro, D. A. Ross, K. V. Elisevich, and B.
J. Smith, "A direct brain interface based on event-related potentials,"
*IEEE Trans Rehabil Eng,* vol. 8, pp. 180-5, 2000.

[48] Laura Bailey. New cochlear implant could improve hearing .
*2008*Available:
http://www.umich.edu/news/index.html?Releases/2006/Feb06/r02060
6a

[49] J. J. Vidal, "Toward direct brain-computer communication," *Annu
Rev Biophys Bioeng,* vol. 2, pp. 80-157, 1973.

[50] J. R. Wolpaw and D. J. McFarland, "Control of a two-dimensional
movement signal by a noninvasive brain-computer interface in humans,"
*Proc Natl Acad Sci,* vol. 101, 2004.

[51] J. P. Donoghue, "Connecting cortex to machines: recent advances in
brain interfaces," *Nat Neurosci,* vol. 5, pp. 8-1085, 2002.

[52] S. P. Levine, J. E. Huggins, S. L. BeMent, R. K. Kushwaha, L. A.
Schuh, M. M. Rohde, E. A. Passaro, D. A. Ross, K. V. Elisevich, and B.

J. Smith, "A direct brain interface based on event-related potentials," *IEEE Trans Rehabil Eng,* vol. 8, pp. 180, 2000.

[53] A. B. Schwartz, "Cortical neural prosthetics," *Annu Rev Neurosci,* vol. 27, pp. 487-507, 2004.

[54] B. Kleber and N. Birbaumer, "Direct brain communication: neuroelectric and metabolic approaches " *Cogn Process,* vol. 6, pp. 65-74, 2005.

[55] N. Weiskopf, K. Mathiak, S. W. Bock, F. Scharnowski, R. Veit, W. Grodd, R. Goebel, and N. Birbaumer, "Principles of a brain-computer interface (BCI) based on real-time functional magnetic resonance imaging (fMRI) " *IEEE Trans Biomed Eng,* vol. 51, pp. 70-966, 2004.

[56] E. C. Leuthardt, G. Schalk, J. R. Wolpaw, J. G. Ojemann, and D. W. Moran, "A brain-computer interface using electrocorticographic signals in humans," *J Neural Eng,* vol. 1, pp. 63-71, 2004.

[57] B. Graimann, J. E. Huggins, S. P. Levine, and G. Pfurtscheller, "Toward a direct brain interface based on human subdural recordings and wavelet-packet analysis," *IEEE Trans Biomed Eng,* vol. 51, pp. 62-954, 2004.

[58] E. E. Sutter, "The brain response interface: communication through visually induced electrical brain responses," *Journal of Microcomputer Application,* vol. 15, pp. 31-45, 1992.

[59] N. Birbaumer, A. Kubler, N. Ghanayim, T. Hinterberger, J. Perelmouter, J. Kaiser, I. Iversen, B. Kotchoubey, N. Neumann, and H. Flor, "The thought translation device (TTD) for completely paralyzed patients," *IEEE Trans Rehabil Eng,* vol. 8, pp. 190, 2000.

[60] E. Donchin, K. M. Spencer, and R. Wijesinghe, "The mental prosthesis: assessing the speed of a P300-based brain-computer interface," *IEEE Trans Rehabil Eng*, vol. 8, pp. 174-9, 2000.

[61] G. Pfurtscheller, C. Neuper, and N. Birbaumer, "Human Brain-Computer Interface," in Motor Cortex in Voluntary Movements: A distributed system for distributed functions"," *CRC Press*, pp. 367-401, 2005.

[62] G. Mason and G. E. Birch, "A brain-controlled switch for asynchronous control applications," *IEEE Trans Biomed Eng*, vol. 47, pp. 1297-307, 2000.

[63] R. Scherer, G. R. Muller, C. Neuper, B. Graimann, and G. Pfurtscheller, "An asynchronously controlled EEG-based virtual keyboard: improvement of the spelling rate," *IEEE Trans Biomed Eng*, vol. 51, pp. 979-84, 2003.

[64] N. Neumann, A. Kubler, J. Kaiser, T. Hinterberger, and N. Birbaumer, "Conscious perception of brain states: mental strategies for brain-computer communication," *Neuropsychologia*, vol. 41, pp. 1028-36, 2003.

[65] Wilhelmwundt.com. *2008*Available: http://www.wilhelmwundt.com/

[66] Omar Khaleefa, "Who Is the Founder of Psychophysics and Experimental Psychology," *American Journal of Islamic Social Sciences*, vol. 16,

[67] Marvin L. Minsky. *2008*Available: http://machineslikeus.com/People/Minsky_Marvin.html

---

[68] Javier Pajares, Cesáreo Hernández-Iglesias and Adolfo López-Paredes. (2004, 31-Mar-2004). Modelling learning and R&D in innovative environments: A cognitive multi-agent apporach. *Journal of Artificial Societies and Social Simulation 7(2),*

[69] D. L. Hoffman and T. P. Novak, "Bridging the racial divide on the Internet," pp. 390-391, 1998.

[70] L. A. Jackson, "Social psychology and the digital divide," *The 1999 Conference of the Society for Experimental Social,* 1999.

[71] Sax, L. J., Ceja, M., & Teranishi, R. T., "Technological preparedness among entering freshmen: the role of race, class and gender," *Journal of Educational Computing Research,* vol. 24, pp. 363-383,

[72] J. W. Schofield. (1997, Computers and classroom social processes: A review of the literature. *Social Science Computer Review 15*pp. 27-39.

[73] Jackson, L. A., Ervin, K. S., Gardner, P. D., & Schmitt, N. (2001, Gender and the internet: Women communicating and men searching. *Sex Roles 44(5),* pp. 363-379.

[74] Jackson, L. A., Ervin, K. S., Gardner, P. D., & Schmitt, N. (2001, The racial digital divide:Motivational, affective and cognitive correlates of internet use. *Journal of Applied Social Psychology 31*pp. 2019-2046.

[75] Peter H. Lindsay and Donald A. Norman, "Human Information Processing: An Introduction to Psychology," *American Journal of Psychology,* vol. 110, pp. 635-641, 1997.

[76] Kellogg,Wendy A. and Richards, John T., "the human factors of information on the Internet," *Advances in Human –computer Interaction,* vol. 5, pp. 1-36, 1995.

[77] Lewis, Nielsen, Landauer and Virzi, "Sample sizes for usability studies: Additional considerations," *Human Factors,* vol. 36, pp. 368-378,

[78] Molich, R.,Bevan, N.,Butler, S., Curson, I., KIndlund,E.,Kirakowski,J., & Miller, D., "Comparative evaluation of usability tests," in 1998,

[79] Sarah Kershaw, "Hooked on the Web: Help is on the way," December 01, 2005.

[80] C. Presno, "Taking the byte out of internet anxiety: Instructional techniques that reduce computer/internet anxiety in the classroom," *J. Educ. Comput. Res.,* vol. 18, pp. 147-161, 1998.

[81] LUT. Fact and figure. *2008*Available: http://www.lut.fi/en/lut/admissions/lut/Documents/international_stu dies_guide_07.pdf

# Legal Notice

The idea and opinion expressed in this thesis are my own or those of others which I have wished to express. Works are cited and due credits are given to author where ideas were not mine. Apologies where credit is not given due to the unknown source of an article and author, please contact me to give credit. No part of this thesis may be reproduced in any form without my prior consent. The references in this thesis were generated using http://www.refworks.com. To download the complete list of references visit http://www.kalwar.com.np/ref.html.

# Appendices: Appendix 1

| Date | Selected Events |
|---|---|
| 1970 | APRANET, US Defense Department network in use. Software and theories were tested for The Internet |
| 1974 | First Small Computer |
| 1975 | Establishment of Telecom industry, Telstra in 1995 |
| 1977 | Wide use of Fiber Optics, PC was introduced. |
| 1979 | Start of USENET, Students using UNIX computers communicate with other students in UNIX community. |
| 1981 | IBM starts selling Personal Computers |
| 1983 | CD was introduced. |
| 1986 | NSFNET created for the connection of supercomputers around USA. |
| 1989 | WWW invented by Tim Berners-Lee |
| 1992-1995 | Wide use of WWW, 5 million machines on the Internet worldwide. |
| 1997 | Protocol, WAP developed to allow access to The Internet through wireless devices including mobile phones. |
| 2000 | 30 million domain name registered on WWW, more email than postal mail in the US. |
| 2001 | .com boom, 8 million web pages appears every day. |
| 2002-2007 | Computer Glitch, Y2K problems, Digital TV broadcasting Started. |
| 2015-Future | Human Behavior on the Internet (*HBI*) Are we going towards cognitive network, cognitive radio and building new user interfaces for humans? |

# Appendix 2

## Usability Test Observation Coding Form

| Participants Id | Verbal Behaviors | Strongly Positive Comment |
|---|---|---|
| 1 | | Questions |
| | Non Verbal Behaviors | Smiling/Laughing/Happy |
| | | Evidence of Impatience |
| 2 | Verbal Behaviors | |
| | Non Verbal Behaviors | Rubbing head/eyes/neck |
| 3 | Verbal Behaviors | Strongly Positive Comment |
| | | Questions |
| | | Stated Frustrations |
| | Non Verbal Behaviors | Smiling/Laughing/Happy |
| | | Surprised/Unexpected |
| | | Furrowed brow/Concentration |
| | | Evidence of Impatience |
| | | Leaning in close to screen |
| | | Rubbing head/eyes/neck |
| 4 | Verbal Behaviors | Question |

| | | | |
|---|---|---|---|
| | | Stated Confusion |
| 5 | **Non Verbal Behaviors** | Frowning/Grimacing/Unhappy |
| | | Surprised/Unexpected |
| | | Leaning in close to screen |
| | **Verbal Behaviors** | Suggestion for improvement |
| | | Question |
| | **Non-verbal Behaviors** | Smiling/Laughing/Happy |

# Appendix 3

Cognitive brain OSI model diagram.

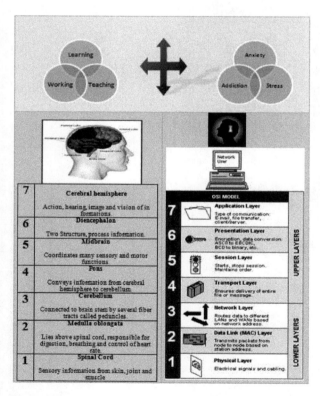

Figure 21: Cognitive brain OSI model (CBOM). Seven parts of human brain are illustrated on the left; similarly, seven layers of the OSI model are illustrated on the right. At the top, human behavior is shown, for example, anxiety, learning and depression among others.

# Appendix 4

You are asked to participate in this task for the research work on the topic "Human behavior on the Internet" conducted by author.

Date: _____          Task #:_____

Start Time: _____          End Time: _____

1.      Find the picture on the Internet with name "human behavior on the Internet_scope.jpg".

2.      Download the picture "human behavior on the Internet_scope.jpg" in the system and upload it again with different name on the Internet

3.      Visit the social networking web site such as (Face book, hi5, My Space, Orkut, Linked in etc) and to create a profile (only one) with name "hbi_study". Also, upload the picture "human behavior on the Internet_scope.jpg".

**Rating**

How easy or difficult the task was? (1=strongly disagree, 3=neither agree nor disagree, 5=strongly agree).

1         2         3         4              5

Easy                                       Difficult

## Appendix 5

The graphs for each of the responses of an item in these questionnaires are recorded and shown below:

1. It is easy to use the Internet.          2. I cannot find what I am looking for on the Internet

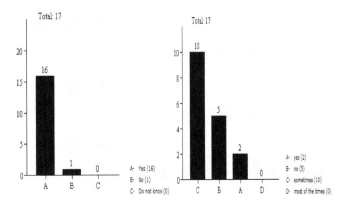

Figure1: Majority of humans think it is easier for them to use the Internet and they sometimes cannot find what they are looking on the Internet.

3   I feel anxious when Internet is not working. 4 My anxiety about internet
bothers me when I have to wait long for a web page to appear.

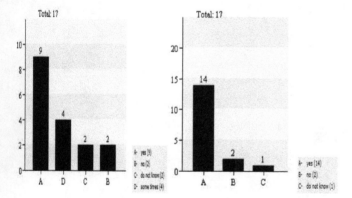

Figure 2: Majority of humans feels anxious when the Internet is not working.
Majority of humans feel anxious when they have to wait longer for a web page
to appear on the Internet.

5 I know what the Internet is.   6 How much you have used the Internet?

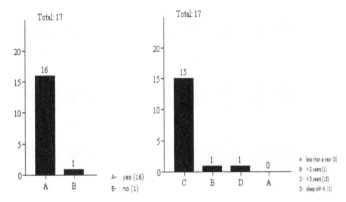

Figure 3: Majority of humans knows the term "internet". Majority of humans have accessed the Internet for more than five years.

7 I visit Face book, hi5, MySpace, Orkut etc.  8 I am uncomfortable using the
Internet

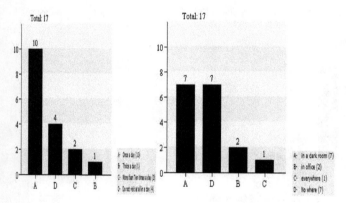

Figure 4: Majority of humans have visit Face book, hi5, MySpace once a day.
Half of the humans feel uncomfortable of using the Internet in a dark room and
half do not feel uncomfortable anywhere or in any environmental setup.

9-Best thing I like being in the Internet

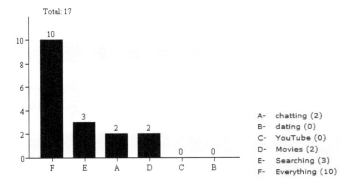

Figure 5: Most of the humans feel comfortable of using the Internet services for example movies, chatting, searching etc.

The **QS2** using the internet consisted of ten items. The responses from the participants were recorded and are shown below in graph.

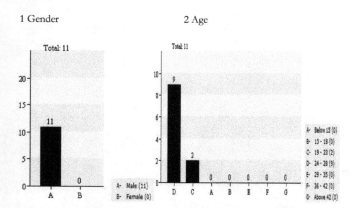

1 Gender          2 Age

Figure 6: Demographic details about Gender and Age of the participants.

3 Marital Status                         4 Occupation

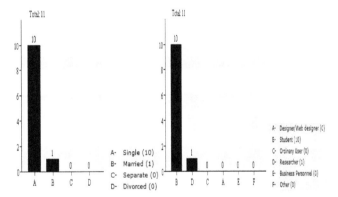

Figure 7: Demographic details about marital status and occupation of the participants.

5 How can the Internet be useful for meeting new people?  6 How long do
you use the Internet?

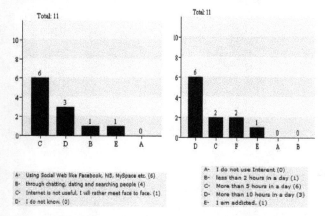

Figure 8: Most of the participants think the Internet can be more useful in
meeting new human using social web pages. On the right hand side of the
graph, Most of the participants use the Internet more than five hours a day.

7 What is the state of mind while using the Internet?  8 Do you lose track of time when using the Internet?

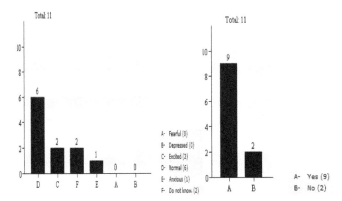

Figure 9: Most of the participants think there state of the mind while using the Internet is normal. Most of the participants loose track of the time when using the Internet.

9 Number of addicted person known    10 Number of people who have felt
anxiety or stress while on the Internet

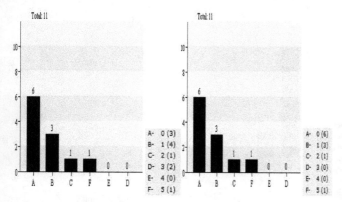

Figure 10: Majority of the participants knows at least one addicted person on
the Internet. On the right hand side of graph, Majority of the participants
answered very few human who have felt anxiety or stress while on the Internet.

# Evaluation of the Thesis

Master of Science work of Santosh Kalwar

Human behavior on the Internet

The work was evaluated on the following basis:

| | |
|---|---|
| Theoretical result | 5 |
| Empirical result (practical) | 4 |
| Autonomy and originality | 5 |
| Coherency and carefulness | 3 |
| Linguistic form | 4 |
| Use of literature | 3 |

**Measure Scale**

1: sufficient

2: satisfactory

3: good

4: very good

5: excellent

**Overall:**          4 *Very good*

## Other perspectives:

The objective of work was to study the human behavior on the Internet. The work done for the thesis includes versatile and challenging literature review. The empirical part of the thesis provides a new model for the study and an analysis of implemented user study. The depth of the review is more than sufficient for the purpose of the M.Sc thesis. However, the depth of the study also in some parts leads to a significant drop in the overall coherence.

The author has designed and implemented a new model for the human behavior on the Internet. The work related to this thesis has already provided scientific contribution as one IEEE journal article has been accepted and 1-2 additional publications are in the process. These articles show that this work has potential. However, the presentation of the actual empirical results is limited and more work should be carried out in this part. Otherwise, the presented new theoretical results provide excellent starting point for future work. The author has developed the research settings and the methodology, even developing a new approach, by himself and thus has presented extraordinary level of independent, autonomy and originality. The thesis contains evaluation section and furthermore the answers to the research setting hypothesis have been evaluated. Future work section is also provided. Text is nicely written and it is easy to read. The work fulfils the requirement for the thesis.

We evaluate work as *Very good* (4)

Lappeenranta, Finland 3.12.2008

Jari Porras                                    Kari Heikkinen

Professor                                      Dr. Sc. (Tech)

Department of Information Technology

Lappeenranta University of Technology

Finland